A Barrister in the Far East

A Barrister in the Far East

Duncan McNeill: Memoirs of Extraterritoriality
in China, Hongkong and Japan (1891-1926)

By my Great-Grandfather Duncan McNeill of Colonsay

T.M. Thorp

© Teresa Thorp 2021

All rights reserved. No part of this publication may be reproduced, stored in a retrieval system, or transmitted in any form or by any means, electronic, mechanical, photocopying, recording or otherwise, without prior permission of the editor, Teresa Thorp.

Paperback: 978-1-80227-776-0
Hardcover: 978-1-80227-778-4
eBook: 978-1-80227-777-7

Dedicated to . . .

My Beloved Mother
Mrs. Teresa Thorp (Paton - McNeill of Colonsay)

Duncan McNeill of Colonsay

Duncan McNeill, born Kensington 19 August 1864, was the first son of Malcolm McNeill, formerly of the army and subsequently of the Civil Service, and Clare Elizabeth Buchanan of Edinburgh. He was educated at Charterhouse, Surrey 1877-83, before being admitted to Corpus Christi as a Scholar. (Corpus Christi 1883-7). He matriculated (registered as a member of the University of Oxford) on 19 October 1883, aged 19, and was made a scholar. He took his BA in 1887. He took a 2nd in Classical Moderations (the first public exams) in 1884 and a 2nd in Literae Humaniores (Classics) in 1887. He graduated B.A. in 1887. He was called to the Bar at the Inner Temple in 1889 and from the beginning of 1891, practised in Extra-territorial Courts throughout the Far East for thirty-five years. He was Acting Crown Advocate in Shanghai 1901-1902.

Duncan's son, John McNeill of Colonsay, was the last Crown Advocate in Shanghai from 1939-1942.

Acknowledgements

There are many to thank for their support, first and foremost the Paton and McNeill of Colonsay families. I am also most grateful for access to archives in the British Library and for the searches conducted by Mr. Julian Reid, The Archivist, Corpus Christi College, Oxford; and Ms. Anna Sander of Oxford University's College Archives.

A Barrister in the Far East

I was called to the Bar in 1889 and went abroad very soon afterwards. For thirty-five years, from the beginning of 1891, I practised in Extra-territorial Courts. As we shall probably, before long, see the end of a system that has been in force ever since our country came into direct relations with the alien cultures of China and Japan, I think that perhaps this record, which covers the period of its decline, may be of interest to the international legal fraternity. Although some years may elapse before H.B.M Supreme Court for China goes the way of H.B.M Court for Japan, it is tolerably certain that no young barrister or solicitor commencing practice in Shanghai in 1930 will be able to report in 1950 that a British Court still exists there.

Most people have a general idea of what Extra-territoriality (or Ex-territoriality or Ex-trality) means; but I may as well state here that, in countries which have by Treaty conceded extra-territorial privileges to British subjects, such persons are amenable only to the law of

England administered by British officials. The subjects of other countries having similar Treaties enjoy, of course, the like immunity from local jurisdiction. It is a typically Chinese system. Chinese jurisdiction applies to universal matters but, as we shall see, established Treaties provide us with much free rein to govern private disputes.

I landed in Yokohama on the 3rd January, 1891, having purchased a half share in the business of Ambrose Berry Walford, a barrister who had been practising in Japan for two or three years as the successor of a Mr. Montague Kirkwood. This gentleman had been appointed an adviser to the Judicial Department of the Japanese Government, which was at that time engaged in drafting new codes of law with the assistance of experts of many nationalities. One of these, I may mention, was the late Sir Francis Piggott, who for some years was Chief Justice in Hong Kong. The practice was good in quality, though hardly big enough to be shared. Walford, however, had some private means and considered that, as the Order in Council creating H.B.M Court for Japan offered no obstacle to partnerships between barrister and barrister, or between barrister and solicitor, the advantage of being able to take an occasional holiday amply compensated for a reduction of income. I was not in the same position for I would have no income apart from my profession for some time and, as will be seen later, my adventure, regarded from a pecuniary point of view, was not very successful. This was due to circumstances which could not have been foreseen, and in particular to a fall of the yen from 3/8 in 1891 to about 2/-, which reduced the sterling value of estimated income of £700 by nearly one half. But I shall return to this subject later; and I will pass now to my professional life in Yokohama.

The British Court in Yokohama, known as H.B.M. Court for Japan, was really a branch of H.B.M. Supreme Court for China, Japan and Corea at Shanghai, to which an appeal lay from its judgments. Its jurisdiction extended over all British subjects in Japan and with regard to all matters except divorce, so that a practitioner might be proving a will one day and on the next be fighting a collision case or defending a person accused of larceny.

Fortunately for me, I had been very well trained in the chambers of Alexander Young, the eldest son of the well-known Scottish judge, Lord Young. He had a good court and chamber practice and I saw a great deal of business of different kinds which included some important conveyancing and a certain amount of Company drafting. Young had a remarkable knowledge of case law and a great dislike of textbooks except as guides to the authorities. His pleadings and opinions were admirable and he was a first class conveyancer, but his impetuosity detracted somewhat from his effectiveness in Court.

He always knew his cases thoroughly and was too apt to interrupt counsel on the other side when they went wrong on their facts. I soon realized how much judges disliked his interventions and have tried to profit by his example in my own practice. The time I spent in Young's chambers, both as a pupil and after my call, was of the greatest value to me, as he took a special interest in my education on account of our mutual connection with Edinburgh and the Scottish Bench, and showed it by always keeping me busy. Amongst other work, I drafted all the conveyancing documents necessary for putting in order the affairs of a large trust estate, which had been managed in a very irregular way by dishonest solicitors: just in time too, for they failed not long afterwards and many of their clients lost money. I also got up for Young a case of much interest to us both as fishermen. This case (*Tilbury v Silva*) concerned a claim of copyholders to fish with nets, and we won it for the defendant both in the court of first instance and in the Court of Appeal.

It was entirely against Young's advice that I went to Japan: he pressed me strongly with the argument that, if I stayed on with him, he would probably take silk in a few years and part of his junior practice might come to me. It was lucky for me that I did not heed his counsel, for he died very soon after I was established in Yokohama. But I have always attributed to his training any success which I have had in my profession, and I wish to record here my gratitude.

I have mentioned my work in Young's chambers, because I can say, judging from long experience, that when I came to Japan I was better qualified to practice there or in China than any other man I have known – to this extent at least, that I had been better taught. The Court procedure was, of course, quite new to me, as it was governed by rules made by the Chief Justices in Shanghai, the White Book being only followed in cases for which the rules did not provide. And I had little knowledge of Admiralty, Probate or Criminal Law.

Our bar was a very small one and consisted of ourselves and two other barristers, Litchfield and Lowder, each of whom practised alone. Litchfield, a sensible man and a sound lawyer, was Crown Prosecutor. His disposition was placid and, as he had not been home for twenty years, his methods seemed to me to be rather old-fashioned. Lowder was much older than the rest of us. He had been British Consul in Yokohama many years before, and after taking steps to be called to the Bar during his home leaves, had resigned his post. The Government, so I was told, was rather annoyed with him; for he had been accorded special facilities for carrying out what was assumed to be an intention of making himself a more efficient public servant. Lowder and Kirkwood had been rivals, while the latter was still in practice.

Walford was a very clear thinker and the best lawyer of us all, but a certain dryness in his court manner prevented him from being a really good advocate except in technical cases. The smaller firms generally employed Litchfield or ourselves, but I think that Litchfield, owing to his long residence, probably had more to do with people's private affairs than we had.

Among our more important clients were the Hongkong and Shanghai Bank and Messrs. Jardine Matheson & Co., both of whom, as it happened, were clients of the firm, which I afterwards joined in Shanghai. The Nippon Yusen Kaisha, the well-known steamship company, paid us an annual retainer of Yen 2000 to cover everything except court work, and the Mitsui firms gave us whatever business they had.

My recollection of practice in Yokohama during my first year is that I was always fully occupied. We had several cases in Court, but Walford attended to most of these while I was learning the practice and trying my hand at such unfamiliar work as writing letters of demand and taking proofs of witnesses. We also brought out a Company or two, registering them under the Companies' Ordinances of Hong Kong. In the case of one of them, the promoters had no money to pay our fees so we took them in Founders' Shares, which we soon sold at a good profit.

My first court case concerned a sealing schooner. By agreement between the British and Russian Governments, a certain zone adjacent to a group of islands, known as the Commander Islanders and lying off the coast of Kamchatka, was reserved to Russia; and it was provided that British sealers found within the zone and suspected of poaching should be sent to the nearest British Court (H.B.M. Court for Japan) for trial and, if found guilty, should have their schooners confiscated. The captain of a Canadian schooner, sent in under the provisions of this agreement, asked me to defend him, and the experience which I gained in doing so convinced me that there is a good deal to be said in favour of the fusion of the two branches of the legal profession, and of the conduct of a case in court by the man who has seen the witnesses in chambers. Both the master and the members of his crew were very intelligent men, but too much pre-occupied at first with the importance of saving the ship in which all their money was invested to appreciate the necessity of putting a rational story before the court. For example, they were inclined to think that when captured they had lost their bearings and did not know where they were. But they had been arrested too close to the islands to make it possible, as I pointed out, for the court to accept this view. So, on reconsideration, it was unanimously decided that they were well aware of the position of the ship within the zone, but were merely sailing across it in order to get to other sealing grounds. Then came the question of a raw sealskin, which was found on board, and for a long time there was considerable diversity of opinion as to how, when and where the seal to which it had belonged was killed. At last it was settled that on the evening before the arrest, while the schooner was still outside the zone, the chief hunter had been stalking a sea otter asleep on the water and that a seal had bobbed up beside him and met its fate. For all I know to the contrary this tale was true: they thrashed it out in private and brought it to me as part of my instructions. So at least I had an intelligible defence, and there were two other points in the schooner's favour, namely, she was heading off shore when sighted, and that she made no attempt to escape. In the result, the ship was released and the judge paid compliments to the master and crew on the straightforward way in which they had given their evidence; and so they had. But I can say, for my part, that while I have no reason to doubt their veracity, their story wanted a good deal of putting into shape.

Almost immediately afterwards I had another similar case, about which I felt much less hopeful. A notorious old seal poacher had been caught close to the islands and put up the same defence – that he was sailing across the zone. Although he had no skins on board his reputation would have ruined him but for the circumstance that the weather was and, for some days, had been, too bad to permit the launching of a boat. So he got the benefit of the doubt; and I should not omit to mention that the Russian officers played the game and did not dispute the weather conditions. I have no idea what my client's intentions were, but the public certainly regarded him as a very lucky man.

The judge of the Court at the beginning of 1891 was Mr. (afterwards Sir Nicholas) Hannen, a half-brother of Lord Hannen. He only remained, however, for a short time, being transferred to Shanghai as Chief Justice.

From the earliest days of the courts for China and Japan the rule had been that the Crown Advocate at Shanghai was appointed acting Judge in Japan; in the case of any temporary vacancy, the Judge in Japan in like manner acting as Chief Justice at Shanghai when required. In each case the substantive appointment came in due course to the man who had held the acting one. Thus, the Supreme Court at Shanghai had the advantage of being presided over by a judge who had not only practised there at the Bar but had also a certain amount of judicial experience. Such were the careers of Sir Nicholas Hannen, of his predecessor, Sir Richard Rennie, and of his successor Sir Hiram Wilkinson.

Hannen was succeeded by Mowatt, who had been attached to the Shanghai Supreme Court as Registrar and Police Magistrate. I suppose that the Crown Advocate (Wilkinson) could have had the appointment if he had desired it. He was Judge in Japan later, but, no doubt at the time, preferred to continue his private practice and train his son to be his successor in office. Mowatt occupied the bench throughout the remainder of my time in Japan. He was careful and painstaking but not a brilliant judge.

Early in the Spring of 1892 Walford went home for the year's holiday to which each of us was entitled under our five years' agreement of partnership. By that time, I knew most of our regular clients pretty well; but I was too new, and really, at twenty-seven, too young to have their complete confidence. Walford said all he could in my favour, but during his absence (I think) they only came to me when they were obliged to do so. Still I got a certain amount of work and, in particular, one very important piece of business, which made the year 1892 a memorable one for me. The P. & O. SS. "Ravenna" sunk the Japanese cruiser "Chishima-Kan", in the Inland Sea and nearly all the crew of the warship were drowned. The Japanese government sued the company in the British Court and I was instructed by Kirkwood to act for them. I drew the pleadings in the collision case and also in an action by the relatives of the crew. Both of these cases went ultimately to the Privy Council, the first on a technical point – whether a counter-claim would lie in H.B.M Court for Japan against the Emperor. This was decided against the Company and the case was settled privately. The other case was disappointing. After much consideration, and after the Company had refused to allow our claim to be treated as a test case, we joined all the relatives – some fifty or sixty – in one action. Mowatt dismissed our claim on the ground of misjoinder of parties, but by the time that our appeal had reached the Supreme Court in Shanghai a case decided in the High Court of Justice in England had approved a similar joinder of plaintiffs, and Hannen reversed Mowatt. Before we got to the Privy Council this decision had been upset by the Court of Appeal; so after wasting much time and money we had to accept defeat. It was unlucky for us that the judgment of the Court of Appeal was delivered in time to prevent our relying on the case, which had helped us so well in Shanghai. In the counterclaim appeal, Sir Richard Webster (Lord Alverstone) led for us, and Sir Robert Finlay (Lord Finlay) for the Company.

Great Britain was the only country, which maintained a Court in Japan, the other Treaty Powers being content to entrust judicial authority to consular representatives, who sometimes appeared to consider that their ordinary duty of protecting their nationals included shielding them from the strict rigour of their country's laws. By way of illustration I will mention a case which occurred soon after my arrival and which caused acute friction between the British and American communities. An American naval officer had a feud with a British subject, an exchange broker, on account of unwelcome attentions paid by the latter to the officer's wife, and, as the broker drove along the Bund in his dog-cart with a friend beside him, the American chased him with a revolver and fired several shots which might have well killed the friend or a Japanese groom, but which happened to take effect on the broker. He died the same night and the entire British community attended his funeral. A prosecution before the U.S. Consul General and his assessors followed, and Litchfield was officially requested to represent the U.S. People. The accused was defended by one of his own countrymen, a professor of law in Tokio University, who in addressing the Court confined himself to denunciations of the deceased man and his surviving friends, mingled with quotations from Shakespeare and other well-known writers, and did not touch on the only matter open to argument, namely whether the provocation was sufficiently recent to reduce the crime from murder to manslaughter. The case that he set up and which the accused supported by his evidence was that his client was trying to miss and not to hit the deceased: he merely wanted to induce him to pull up, and get down to take a licking. The Court, however, was of a different opinion and gave judgment to the effect that the shooting was intentional, but that it was amply justified by the provocation received and that the accused must accordingly be acquitted. As it is clear that the object which defending counsel and the Court had in view was to protect the accused from any sentence which might involve the loss of his commission, I think that I prefer the decision of the Court, which simply put all law and evidence aside, to the suggestion of the professor that death was due to accident. Litchfield conducted the prosecution with good sense and dignity in spite of the brow-beating to which he was constantly subjected by the Court. I doubt if the dead man desired that another should swing for him; but no provocation, however great, could justify the firing at three men in a fast moving dog-cart on the chance of hitting one. The acquittal gave rise to very bitter feeling and Americans were practically ostracized from British society for some time.

In 1892, the Hongkong and Shanghai Bank imported a new accountant and began a great general cleaning up, in the course of which several prominent social figures went under and a certain amount of fraud was exposed. I did not find the public examination of debtors either interesting or pleasant. It requires no particular art to extort admissions of irregularity from ruined and broken men.

Shortly before Walford's return in 1893 I was advised that the death of a leading British lawyer in Kobe might make it worth our while to open a branch there, so I travelled by sea to that port in order to survey the ground. By way of a start I hung up a board with our names outside a friend's office, called on the representatives of the Hongkong and Shanghai Bank and Messrs. Jardine Matheson and Co., and talked in the club about our possible intentions. But nothing came of it as Walford threw cold water on the scheme. The Kobe business went into the hands of Litchfield who brought out a partner, and established him there. This barrister continued to practise in Kobe for many years, having taken a Japanese partner when extra-territoriality was abolished. He did rather well, I believe, as he got a good deal of agency business both from Shanghai and from Hong Kong. Oddly enough, I have been told that he came out straight from the Divorce Courts, where he can hardly have learned much that was of service to him in Japan.

In June 1893, I was married and, during the remainder of the year, most of my time was taken up with the *Chishima-Ravenna* case – interviewing experts, studying charts, and considering the problems of international law arising from the P. & O.'s counterclaim. Our position in regard to this was that the Emperor owned the cruiser and that as he could not be sued in his own courts he could not be liable to a counterclaim in H.B.M Court for Japan. It would have been a gracious act on the part of the Emperor to waive his immunity, but our instructions were to contest the right of counterclaim to the bitter end. In a case of such importance there were naturally a number of interlocutory proceedings in which Walford or I had to appear. Soon after the action had been started we became associated with a Japanese colleague, Mr. Okamura, who had been called to the English bar and had a good practice in his own courts. He was a very agreeable man, but he did not give us any real assistance. Indeed, he was only brought in for the sake of appearances. He signed the pleadings with me.

In 1894, the war between China and Japan broke out and brought us a certain amount of new business. But, by this time, unfortunately, the yen had fallen from 3/8 to 2/- and my wife and I were finding life rather difficult. However, I managed to secure a lectureship on English Law in a large institution (half school, half university) run by a prominent Japanese educationist in Tokio. This engagement took me to the capital three times a week and the salary usefully supplemented my income. The work was not so interesting as I expected it to be, as I was directed to lecture by way of dictation and my pupils, with few exceptions, did not know enough English to take down what I said correctly.

In the same year an event occurred which seriously affected my position. By a treaty concluded between Great Britain and Japan, H.B.M. Court in the last mentioned country was to be abolished at the end of five years. Probably in view of the imminent restoration of their country's full sovereignty, the Japanese began to discard foreign assistance. The Government dismissed many foreign advisers, and the Nippon Yusen Kaisha withdrew our retainer, although they still came to us for advice when they required it. The situation caused me much anxiety, for I had ascertained that it would be impossible for me to practise in Japanese Courts unless I was called to the Japanese bar and, of course, spoke the language perfectly. It was clear that I should have to move on and, accordingly, I began to enquire about a position with some Shanghai firm. None, however, was offering at the moment; so I had to be content to sit still. With assistance from my friends at home I was just able to keep my head above water.

In April 1895, my stay in Yokohama came suddenly to an end. I had already settled to use the year's holiday which was due to me in prospecting new ground, but had not yet fixed upon any definite locality, when the decision was made for me in the following way.

A member of the Hongkong bar who had shared with J.J. Francis, Q.C. the bulk of the leading business, was appointed a Puisne Judgeship in Singapore, and Francis thought that his practice would suffer if he had no opponent who could put up something like a fight against him. The man who was going away was not his match, but he could always give clients a run for their money, and none of the remaining men were, in his opinion, able to do that. So he wrote and suggested to Lowder that he should move to Hong Kong. Lowder did not care to leave Japan and accordingly passed on the suggestion to Walford, who turned it down for reasons of health, and to Litchfield who did the same. Walford then advised me that, as there was at any rate an opening, I might as well go and see what I could do to fill it, even if I could not expect to meet Francis' requirements. I fell in with the idea, left my wife and child in Japan, and sailed in April for Hong Kong. I reckoned that I should at least be able to pay my way for a time as Walford had thought it right, in the circumstances, to return part of my purchase money, and I hoped that my continuing income from the partnership would suffice – as it did – for my wife's needs.

The step that I took was, no doubt, a hasty one; but I had to break some new ground and, in the absence of any vacancy in Shanghai, Hongkong really offered the best chances to a barrister.

T.M. Thorp

So far I have dealt only with my work, but, before I quit Japan, I should make some reference to my life outside of the office. During my first year, and until he went home in 1892, I lived with my partner, Walford. He had a charming bungalow on the Bluff looking sheer down into the sea – I think it disappeared, or, at any rate the garden did, in the 1923 earthquake. We rode on most days before breakfast round the hill paths or on the racecourse, and on Sundays went further afield to some pleasant place where we could lunch. Often we formed part of a cheerful crowd – "The Knights of Asia" – whose objective was usually Kamakura (15 miles distant by hill paths) where there was a large semi-foreign hotel, and we could get a change and a bath. Most of us used to turn our ponies over to our *"bettou"* (grooms) and go home by rail, as our mounts were not equal to the return journey. In summer, Walford generally took for the month of June a large room in a Japanese seaside hotel, bringing his cook and boys down with him and making it a temporary home. An 8 o'clock train brought us to Yokohama before 10. He could only get this room for June as, after that month, it was occupied by a Japanese prince. It was of exceptional size – 50 mats – an ordinary room being of six or eight mats. Rooms in a Japanese house are always covered as to the floor with mats of identical dimensions, namely six feet by three feet, and about three inches in depth. Our room easily slept six people and left ample free space in which we could dine a dozen or more. The bathing, before breakfast and in the evenings, was delicious; and the hotel had a splendid bath house where you could wash the salt out of your hair. On Sundays, when we always had visitors, we practically lived in the water.

In winter, I played football (Association) regularly on Saturdays and represented Yokohama in the Annual Interport matches in Kobe. We had some very good men, especially one back who would have got his "Blue" easily at either Oxford or Cambridge: one or two forwards were also up to that standard. In the spring and autumn, I rowed every evening, and, as I had belonged to a rowing college at Oxford and had been well coached, I won a fair number of prizes. My best performance was the stroking of a pair at the Yokohama Coming of Age Regatta when we beat our competitors from Kobe and Hongkong by many lengths.

A friend of mine shared with me a small yacht – I don't know her rating but she had about 1 ½ tons of lead on her keel and carried a lot of sail – and we had good sport racing her in summer. In those days there was only one outward mail a week and as Friday was mail-day, Saturday was comparatively free. Accordingly, every Saturday there was a whole day race for yachts of different classes starting at 8.30 and finishing at about 5 o'clock. As the summer breeze was steady from the S.E., races were always sailed over the same course – out along the few hundred yards of breakwater with spinnakers set if you could find room, a beat down the bay to Yokosuka, the Japanese naval station, and a run home. The run was a tedious business on a hot day but, towards the end of the course, boats had to haul round a buoy outside the harbour and beat in to the finishing line. We had no real competitor in our own class so we amused ourselves by trying to outsail big yachts and often succeeded in doing so. They did not like it.

In winter, Walford and I dined out a good deal and often had friends in to play whist. Occasionally we had dinner at the club and played bowls afterwards in the bowling alley. There were a few public and private dances and now and then local amateurs or visiting professionals gave a concert or a play in our Public Hall. Both of us went pretty often to Tokio (one hour by rail) for a meal or to spend the night. I was early brought into touch with people there as an uncle of mine had visited Japan in 1889 on the staff of H.R.H the Duke of Connaught, and had made a number of friends who were very civil to me. But in 1891 the Legation staff and British residents in Tokio were divided into two factions, one of which supported Mr. Hugh Fraser the Minister, and the other the First Secretary, the Master of Napier, to whom I had an introduction from my uncle. The Master was away on leave and Walford soon made me acquainted with Mr. Fraser to whose party I became more or less attached. The Master of Napier was succeeded by de Bunsen, a cousin of my fiancée, and he had, as Second Secretary, Spring Rice, whose younger brother was my closest friend at Charterhouse. Both of these men were devoted supporters of their chief who was, however, extremely unpopular with the British mercantile community in Japan, which accused him of wantonly abandoning the prestige gained for Great Britain by his predecessor, Sir Harry Parkes. This Minister, no doubt, did excellent work in the days before Japan decided that she would fall into line with foreign powers, but now that the decision had been made, a different type of diplomatist was better fitted to deal with the new situation. Mr. Fraser's country-men were obstinately opposed to any alteration in the conditions of life to which they were accustomed, and regarded with disfavour anyone who was actively concerned in bringing about a change. The intensity of the feeling against H.M. representative may be illustrated by the account of his funeral, which was published by a Yokohama paper, and contained the following passage:

> "*As might have been expected the attendance on the part of Yokohama residents was in proportion to the popularity of the deceased – extremely limited.*"

Naturally, this coarse insult evoked protests from all decent people. Tokio at this time was the home of several distinguished men, among whom I will name, Milne, the seismologist; Brinkley, famous as an authority on Oriental Art; and Chamberlain, who had lately retired from the unusual position of Professor of Japanese literature in Tokio University, and whose books on Japan are still in the hands of all travellers.

Kirkwood and his wife did a great deal for me in the way of making me acquainted with the staffs of the various foreign legations. At their house also I met interesting visitors from time to time, and among them Curzon, to whom I took an instinctive dislike. I think that he annoyed me by his bad taste in speaking disparagingly of Spring Rice who was an intimate friend of his hosts and a very popular figure in Tokio society.

In August 1891, I went for a month's tour with one of the student interpreters at H.M. Legation. Our intention was to walk as much as possible and to live on Japanese food. We took no servant with us, the serious object of our expedition being to give my friend practice in the spoken language with a view to his approaching examination. Our start was made from Karuizawa, then the summer quarters of the British minister, and, being detained at our hotel for two days by rain, we took a practical step towards ensuring toleration of the almost tasteless Japanese food, which was to be our sole diet for several weeks, by drenching every dish with Worcestershire sauce. This simple measure succeeded even beyond expectation, and we got through our tour without serious inconvenience, although we did not often enjoy a meal for any other reason than that we were very hungry. We began by climbing Asama Yama, the well-known volcano, and then crossed by rail to the west side of the main island. A night's journey in a tiny steamer brought us to Niigata, a decayed Treaty Port with one foreign resident, an Italian. From Niigata we reached Sado, an island which contains the principal gold mines of Japan and is rarely visited by travellers. Returning to the Mainland further south we made our way back eastward through the Hida Mountains (the so-called Alps of Japan) and finally descended the famous Tenryugawa rapids to the railway which brought us home. These rapids were barely passable owing to flood, so we had quite an exciting time. Our friends had told us that we should not be able to endure the native food, but we falsified their prophecies by returning in very good condition.

The trip cost us less than 100 yen (say £20) each including first-class travel by sea and rail, journeys in rickshaws and some small purchases of curios. The explanation of this low figure is that even the best inns charged no more than 50 sen (1/10) for bed, bath, dinner and breakfast, and inferior establishments very much less. One rule had to be steadily adhered to, namely to take what was offered to us and to be content with it. To order anything extra or special was to double our bill. But there was always rice *ad libitum* and therefore no need to go hungry. One Japanese basket each was all our luggage and that meant that we had to have two porters when we were walking and three rickshaws when we were crossing the plains. Sometimes in the mountains our luggage was carried by a pack-horse instead of by coolies. I must make special mention of one man who gave an almost incredible amount of service for an absurdly small sum. He carried a Japanese basket uphill for half a day to our starting point for a mountain climb, walked with us from 4 a.m. to 4 p.m. to the summit (8,000 feet), walked down next day (9 a.m. to 6 p.m.), and finally carried our basket to the place where we had engaged him. He asked for 1 yen (3/8) and we gave him 2 yen to his great delight. We felt rather ashamed, but we could not spoil the market for other travellers.

When Walford went home, in 1892, he let his bungalow and I moved to a small house where I proposed to live after my marriage, which was already arranged for 1893. I shared this house with another man, my partner in the yacht, and as I had all Walford's excellent servants we were very comfortable.

The Hannens were almost next door and we both knew them well and saw much of them. My friend used to pass every weekend with them at Hakone where they had their home in summer. He used to leave Yokohama at noon on Saturday and after a long journey by train and horse-tram and a walk of one and a half hours up the steep Hakone pass, reached his destination. Late hours and a busy day spent in the water or in climbing hills were followed by a return journey to Yokohama, which began at 4 a.m. and ended at 10. These exertions in the great heat of summer I think undermined his health and, in the winter, he nearly succumbed to an attack of enteric.

Of course I had to figure in my kilt at the annual Caledonian Balls and as I never claimed to be an expert reel dancer I found it embarrassing to be obliged to exhibit myself before a ring of spectators of all nationalities. But the standard of dancing was so low that I was looked on as quite a good performer. I knew better, and, so I am sure, did some of the onlookers. Oddly enough the St. George's

Society had never given a ball and did not give one in my time. The expense of these annual entertainments was very heavy as the Scots had to invite practically the whole community. But they were thoroughly enjoyed.

About this time, I had a visit from a connection of mine, Graham Balfour, who was on his way to stay with his cousin R. L. Stevenson in Samoa. Later I received £5 from Balfour with instructions to spend it on Japanese Kimonos for his host. I executed the commission and was rewarded by a most appreciative letter of thanks from R.L.S. who told me that he had entirely discarded European for Japanese dress. Much of my leisure time was spent in getting together fittings for my house and at various Consulate and Legation sales I managed to acquire some very good pieces of furniture which served me throughout my time in the Far East. The Japanese have some excellent varieties of wood, so I had bookcases, etc., made to my order. Japanese hemp carpets compare well with Axminister and are inexpensive. Japanese matting for stairs and passages is hard to beat. Japanese wall papers in imitation of stamped leather, are extremely durable.

I was married in June, 1893, from the British Legation in Tokio where my wife and her father stayed with their cousin de Bunsen, and we spent our honeymoon at Nikko. Early in 1894 we moved to another house situated on the edge of the Bluff Gardens, a tennis club whose grounds were enclosed by beautiful cherry trees, and there, in the spring, our eldest son was born. This was a delightful house, but intensely hot in summer, as indeed all houses and offices were. There were no punkahs in Yokohama in those days, except, I believe, in one house on the Bund. In our office a thermometer on an inside wall registered 95° for many weeks, and no breath of wind reached the northward facing business quarter. It was a great relief to get away to Chusenji where the Kirkwoods had built a charming villa. This place was a whole day's journey from Tokio so that we had to sleep a night in the capital before starting, and, with an amah and baby, the numerous changes were, to say the least, rather trying. We took a train to Utso-no-Miya, a rickshaw to Nikko, and a rickshaw again to the foot of the Chusenji pass. Then we had a long steep climb to the lakeside, the amah and baby being carried in a *kago* (litter). But the coolness and beauty of the place amply repaid us for our trouble. I caught a three pound salmon while I was staying with Kirkwood. He had to make special arrangements with the fishermen, who were very jealous of their rights and as a rule only rowed foreigners about over ground where there was no chance of a fish. These land-locked salmon are very good eating and a ten pound fish was always to be had for a banquet at one of the Legation houses. Many of the foreign Legations had summer quarters at this lovely place, 4,000 feet above the sea, with a splendid lake and exquisite mountain scenery. There was also a Japanese hotel there, but I think that the Kirkwoods were the only people except the diplomats who had a private house at Chusenji.

In the summer of 1894 we had a thrilling experience. The British fleet on the China station, at that time commanded by Sir Edmund Fremantle, had as usual been spending a month or two at Yokohama. Lady Fremantle asked us to go on board the "Alacrity", the Admiral's yacht, to view the Fleet's departure, and we, with her other guests, embarked later on a large tug which a retired British naval officer in Japanese employ had unexpectedly brought alongside. This boat had an awning forward under which the whole party stood. The tug moved out of the harbour and lay to with her engines stopped. Soon the flagship passed us with the Admiral waving his handkerchief from the bridge and the next thing that happened was that, after bumping along the opened ports of the second ship in the line, we found ourselves athwart the course of the remainder of the fleet. There was no panic, the women behaving very well and, but for a moan or two, showing no signs of terror. The nearest cruiser ported her helm a little, our engineer managed to give his engine a turn ahead and all was well. But it was really an awkward situation and had there been a serious collision there must have been a considerable loss of life owing to the awning. We went back to the "Alacrity" for tea and the unlucky naval man made halting apologies for his gross error of judgment in stopping the engines of the tug.

Fremantle, by the way, was an Admiral of the unimpressive pink and white type, but he had plenty of vigour and lived to be over 90. The annual visits of the fleet were more appreciated by the women than by the men of our British community, as the officers were made free of our club and recreation ground and, as was inevitable in such a small place as Yokohama, rather swamped our limited accommodation. But on the whole we liked the navy, although, during my time, an unpleasant incident led to a complete rupture of relations for some months. A member of the Club Committee found a naval officer, who had drunk more than was good for him, making trouble in the bar at about 11 p.m. He approached the man in a friendly way, took his arm, and suggested a stroll in the veranda. The sailor shook him off roughly, saying: "Let me alone d – n you! You're only a b – y merchant anyhow!" This incident was reported to the Captain of the offender's ship, who refused to take any action. The Club Committee then gave notice that in future only captains of men-of-war would be officially invited to use the Club, and that other officers must be proposed and seconded by members like ordinary visitors. The Captain and all his officers thereupon declined to make further use of the Club, and persuaded the other ships to follow their example. They even insisted on the resident surgeon at the British Naval Hospital resigning his membership. This state of things continued until the Admiral (Sir F. Richards) arrived in the "Alacrity", and cheerfully accepted the new and most reasonable arrangement. As I have mentioned no names, I am free to express my regret that the Captain, who was the moving spirit in this discreditable affair, afterwards rose high in his profession. The Committee came out of the business very well and the only person who suffered was the unfortunate naval surgeon. He had everybody's sympathy.

During 1894, we made the acquaintance of a very notable woman – Madam Sannomiya – the wife of the Vice-Master of Ceremonies to the Emperor. It was generally supposed that the Vice-Master, while resident in England, had married the daughter of his landlady, but whatever her origin, it was certainly not aristocratic. She was a kindly and cheerful person, respected and liked by all the members of the diplomatic corps. What was remarkable about her, and proved her to be possessed of great intelligence, was that her official duty was to instruct the Empress and her ladies in waiting in the niceties of court etiquette. Moreover, if a Japanese prince had to be sent abroad on a mission she was attached to his staff to see that he behaved with perfect correctness. It was admitted that she carried out her task admirably and we never heard anyone say an unfriendly word about her. A certain natural dignity and entire freedom from pretentiousness brought her safely through the dangers of a most difficult position. Madam Sannomiya, who had known my uncle well, received us cordially and took us all over one of the Imperial palaces where she gave us tea in its lovely garden.

We often met the Baroness Albert d'Anethan (wife of the Belgian Minister) who was a sister of Rider Haggard and who has since published many novels of which the scene is laid in Japan. Mrs. Fraser, the wife of H.B.M. Minster, also made her mark as a writer after her husband's death. She was a sister of Marion Crawford.

When I went to Japan many foreigners in Yokohama used to be invited to a ball given annually by the Japanese Minster for Foreign Affairs, and in my first year I attended one of these balls. They could also, through their Ministers, obtain invitations to the Imperial Cherry and Chrysanthemum garden parties. But this privilege was withdrawn in 1892 on account of some breach of decorum. I think that the offence was the failure to wear the top hat and frock coat appropriate to the occasion. During most of my time in Japan it was impossible for resident foreigners on any pretext to obtain admission to these Imperial functions. I remember one hard case in connection with this matter. A colonial governor and his wife visited Japan on their way to England and were to be presented to the Emperor at a garden party. A cousin of the wife, himself a man of very good family, was one of the clergy attached to the Anglican Bishop whose headquarters were in Tokio, and great efforts were made by H.M. Legation to obtain a relaxation in his favour of the exclusion rule. The Japanese authorities, however, refused to make any concession.

After I had left Japan in 1895, my wife let our house to two rather interesting Russians, Colonel (afterwards General) Wogack and Baron Gabriel de Gunzburg. The former was military attaché in London for some time, and the latter was said to be the agent of the Grand Dukes in the matter of some timber concessions in Corea which were not remotely connected with the origins of the Russo-Japanese War. Gunzburg came to Shanghai later and visited us there. He was a very sociable man and so eager to keep touch with his friends in the Far East that for many years after he had left China, his coroneted Christmas cards continued to remind them of his good will.

It was a common saying in Yokohama that if a man did not go up Fuji in his first year he would never do so. I proved the truth of this in my own person, for, although I attempted an ascent within the prescribed period, I never got quite to the top. Drenching rain and sleet obliged us to halt (at about 4 a.m.) at the last rest-house and to return at daylight without having reached our objective. My wife went up later from Hakone, the ascent being quite easy and the view of the sunrise from the summit (12,000 feet) being well worth the trouble of a long climb.

I arrived in Hongkong to find the newly appointed judge just about to embark and, with the assistance of friends, I soon secured chambers and hung out my board. There was a good Court Library at my disposal and Walford had allowed me to take some duplicates from our joint stock. I had also ordered from home Smith's Leading Cases and a few text books. So I sat down to wait for briefs. The Chief Justice, Sir Fielding Clark, I had met in Japan; the General, Digby Barker, had been a brother officer of my father; and I had introductions to the heads of the Hongkong and Shanghai Bank, Messrs. Jardine Matheson and Co., Messrs. Butterfield and Swire and others. Moreover, one or two friends of my own age had been transferred from Japan to Hongkong and they took me under their protection and gave me all the recreation I required in the way of tennis, etc. I was fortunately able to engage a cool room in a hotel on the Peak, which I occupied throughout my stay from April to September. Lastly, it happened that Pollock (now Sir Henry, K.C.)

an old school-fellow of mine at Charterhouse, was also practising at the Hongkong Bar. So I cannot say that I felt like a fish out of water for long.

At Hongkong I had again to learn new rules of practice, for the Colonial Ordinance on the subject was based on the Common Law Procedure Act. But practice was now a matter which I could generally leave to the solicitors. It was, however, some time before these people took any notice of me, so I was glad to accept the chance which came along of devilling for another man. A brother-in-law of the barrister who had gone away had taken over most of his pending cases. He was very able and most effective in Court, but he had been called late in life and lacked both training and experience. Such cases as came into his hands were mostly cases in which Francis had been briefed on the other side, and he did not feel that he could cope with the situation by himself. Accordingly, he proposed that I should assist him and offered me what I considered generous terms. Our co-operation had excellent results and we beat Francis in at least one very important case. Of course, so far as the public was concerned, I did not come into the picture. But just at the end of my stay in Hongkong my friend had to go to hospital with fever and a good brief of his was passed on to me by the solicitors. By this time, I was known to most of them. I had the luck to find favour with Francis, who was kind enough to compliment me warmly on my opening in the first case in which I was opposed to him. He had the reputation of bullying junior counsel, but the truth was that he had a great contempt for anyone who asked for the protection of the Court instead of hitting back. He told me once that I had better occupy my time before the next sitting of the Court in refreshing my memory on some elementary point of law and when the judge sat again I was able to say:

> *"My learned friend Mr. Francis, taking full advantage, I think, of his age and position, advised me at the last hearing to refresh my memory on an elementary point of law. I have taken his advice and am now able to cite to your Lordship an authority which establishes the correctness of my views and contradicts those of my friend."*

Francis liked this and was a most valuable friend to me from that day forward. Later on he gave me a good letter to the head of the firm which I was joining in Shanghai – a Roman Catholic like himself – and it was a great pleasure to me, when lunching with him just before I left Hongkong, to reveal myself as the writer of a newspaper article on a subject which concerned him very nearly. In 1894 a serious visitation of Bubonic Plague inflicted great loss on Hongkong. It was finally subdued under the directions of a Committee appointed by the Government, of which Francis was the moving spirit. He returned all his briefs and, for many months, gave his whole time to the work of the Committee for which he also performed the laborious duties of Secretary. But he and the Governor did not get on together so, while Government officials received decorations, Francis was offered an inscribed inkstand as a reward for his services. He returned this unwelcome gift and protested against the unfairness of treating him as a mere secretary. He had the sympathy of the public and also mine. So I wrote a little "Arabian Nights" tale which was published by the leading Hongkong newspaper and was also reprinted in the Straits Times. Francis had been seeking in vain to discover the author of the article, which he had carefully preserved. My secret had been well kept, I am glad to say, or I might have got into trouble over a passage, which particularly pleased Francis. After describing the Governor, Sir William Robinson, as "an Emir called Ibn Rabin (the son of a bird)" I had stated that "Ibn Rabin was tall and of a comely countenance but in nowise skilled in the arts of government".

Besides my work as "devil" I had a few briefs of my own. One was in a criminal case, which I have good reason to remember. My client was one of four or five men accused of kidnapping a girl from Hanoi for sale to a house of ill fame and, while the others were convicted, he was acquitted because I got the right, instead of the wrong, answer to one of those dangerous questions which we are all taught not to ask. The woman had recognised him as one of those whom she had seen at the house to which she was sold. As to the other men, she swore that they had travelled with her on the ship from Hanoi. I consulted the solicitor who had briefed me five minutes before the trial as to whether I could ask her if she had seen my client also on the ship, but he apparently knew nothing about the facts of the case and told me that I could do as I pleased. So I put the question, and I shall never forget the minutes of suspense while I awaited the witness's reply. The Court interpreter only understood Cantonese so he put the question to a Cantonese who spoke the Hanoi dialect and this man passed it on to the woman. The woman answered in her native tongue, the Cantonese answered to the Court interpreter and, at last, it was stated in English that she had never seen my client in Hanoi or on the ship. There was no other evidence to connect him with the kidnapping, so he was acquitted. This was, by the way, my first jury case.

No doubt one reason why I got so little independent work in Hongkong was that the Summary Court, where the Puisne Judge sat, had jurisdiction up to, I think, $1,000. In this court, solicitors had a right of audience and did not as a rule brief counsel. There was a tacit understanding among members of the Bar that they should not go to the Summary Court for less than $50, but I and other junior Counsel would have been very willing to take less as there was not enough Supreme Court work to go round. Fielding Clark, I know, sympathized with our position, but thought that the minimum fee of $50 was much too high.

I had a very happy time in Hongkong: I liked the hot summer; and if I had decided to stay there I daresay I should have become a Colonial "silk" and had the right to appear in that character before the Privy Council though not before any other Court in England. But I was a married man: I had no assurance that the climate of Hongkong would suit my family, and, at any rate, some years must elapse before I was sufficiently established to be able to take a holiday at home without losing my practice. I should mention that the Attorney-General of those days in Hongkong considered that local climatic conditions fully justified disregard of the rule against partnerships between barristers. But this was only his individual opinion and it was never acted on.

When Pollock was passing through Shanghai on his return from home, he heard that a firm of solicitors there wanted a barrister as an assistant. He handed on the news to me and I at once put myself in touch with

Messrs. Dowdall & Hanson who asked me to come to Shanghai and see them. I called on them in June and we fixed matters up. I was to enter their service in September on a three years' agreement at $300 a month with the added privilege of living rent-free in rooms above the office. I stayed with Dowdall for two nights and took a great liking to him; but having experienced the beauties of Japan and Hongkong thought Shanghai a remarkably ugly place. I found out later that it has a charm of its own for anyone who can bear to live out of sight of hills.

My life in Hongkong was free from exciting incident, except a narrow escape from suffocation when some idiot lit a fire of brushwood in the chimney of an abandoned silver mine while I and a companion were climbing up the shaft. It was a very pale and anxious crowd to which we descended through the smoke.

I discovered or imagined that a moustache, which I had been ordered to grow when I became engaged was interfering with my professional prospects by making me appear too young. So I went with a friend to Macao for a day or two and returned with a smooth upper lip which would, I hoped, cause clients to think that I might possibly be older than I looked. Anyhow, I regained my self-respect; for I had been trained to believe that a moustache was an ornament no more appropriate to a barrister's face than a nose-ring.

My young friends in the P. & O. junior mess treated me generously in the matter of bathing parties and Sunday picnics on their big launch. On one occasion, we went some way up the Canton River and killed a good many fish with sticks of dynamite.

I used to row regularly once a week in a four and played a good deal of tennis at a private club in Kowloon called "The Wigwam". During all my six months of residence, I was never allowed to become a normal member of a bathing party or tennis club or to pay anything for my amusements, although I pressed the point strongly. The answer always was that such questions could stand over until I had decided that I was going to live in Hongkong. And, of course, in June I had come to a different decision.

Every Saturday the P. & O. junior mess at the Peak used to ask me to dine or to dine and sleep. The seniors to whom I had introductions were equally kind to me and I look back on my stay in Hongkong as a very pleasant experience, especially after June when my future had been settled and I was sure of covering my expenses through my work as "devil".

I left Hongkong in September and travelled up to Shanghai with Drummond, the senior barrister there, who had been my leader in the case in which I took over my sick friend's brief. He told me that he often went "special" to Hongkong and was very proud of having always beaten Francis whenever they were opposed to one another. We certainly gained our point against him on this occasion, though our task was merely to hand up a losing case on the chance of a settlement. I fancy that Drummond's repeated successes were due to the fact that he always knew his case much better than Francis did. This opinion is based more or less on the fact that I spent three days in almost continuous consultation with him in Hongkong . But I had many opportunities of studying his methods in Shanghai. He had a dignified appearance and an impressive manner, but what chiefly contributed to his success as an advocate was that he never abandoned an argument while there remained the least chance that it had not been fully understood. When a point is very clear to them, even experienced counsel are apt to treat it summarily, with disastrous results. Drummond, I may add, was not at his best in a bad case.

Shortly after I joined the firm in Shanghai my former partner, Walford, was engaged, together with Lowder, in defending a woman who was accused of murdering her husband, the Secretary of the Yokohama Club, by poisoning him with arsenic. After a long trial she was convicted, but H.M. Minister, in exercise of a power given to him by Order in Council, commuted the death sentence into one of penal servitude for life. Walford disappeared from the case early and for a sufficient reason. A letter which the accused wished to inspect was handed to him by the Clerk of the Court and he passed it on to his client; but when documents came to be collected before the Court rose, it could not be found. Search of the accused established the fact that she had concealed it in her sleeve and next day Walford retired from the case, for he considered that the subordinate officials of the Court had been unfairly exposed to the suspicion of having tampered with evidence in the interests of the prisoner, who was a woman of some means. The case was remarkable in several respects and in particular for the inability of the prosecution to suggest any motive for the crime. When no motive can be indicated, circumstantial evidence must be very strong indeed before it will convince a jury that the accused is not at least entitled to the benefit of the doubt. But the woman insisted on clinching the case against her by voluntarily offering alternative explanations (which were all disproved) of the presence of arsenic in her husband's body, and also by imputing murder to an imaginary visitor to Yokohama, a discarded mistress of the dead man, who had written him a passionate letter just before his death. The prosecution established that the letter was written by the accused and thus shattered a defence which, like an alibi, would have been a complete answer to the charge if proved, but if disproved was almost conclusive of guilt. It is difficult not to attribute to Lowder some responsibility for his client's fatal alienations of judgment. If she had refrained from speech and action I do not think that, in view of the absence of motive, she could possibly have been condemned. I knew both husband and wife pretty well as acquaintances.

The firm of Dowdall and Hanson consisted of two solicitors, of whom the senior had been in practice for twenty-five years. He had at one time (in the early seventies) been in partnership with Drummond and later worked with Sir Richard Rennie until the latter was promoted to the bench. When this event took place most of Rennie's business went elsewhere; but Dowdall was able to tell me, when I joined him, that he had got it all back. The most important clients concerned were the Hongkong and Shanghai Bank, Messrs. Jardine Matheson and Co., Messrs, F.D. Sassoon, and the Municipal Council. Hanson, who only came to Shanghai a year or two before I did, was a very capable solicitor. He had been trained in a leading London firm, and was much the best conveyancer of my time. Neither of these men liked Court work though they were both quite useful advocates, being sensible and clear-headed and having no difficulty in arguing a case. But they did not really enjoy that side of their practice and that is why they brought me into their office.

T.M. Thorp

At first my wife and I felt rather lost in Shanghai – a big place compared with Yokohama – the only people we knew being Hannen (now Sir Nicholas) and his family. But that meant a great deal as they were immensely popular and introduced us to all their friends. Before my wife went home in December we had quite a large circle of acquaintances. For exercise, I had as much football, rowing, tennis and golf as I wanted. My salary was small but I still had money coming in to me from Yokohama during 1895 and, as we paid no rent, we managed comfortably enough.

When I first went to Shanghai, H.B.M. Supreme Court for China, Japan and Corea was the only Court there, but before long the Germans had a judicial Vice-Counsel with legal training and the Americans a District Court with a judge. The French also, but not till a good many years later, set up a proper judicial tribunal. In course of time a few German and French lawyers established themselves in practice and a great many Americans of all degrees of competence came across from Manila. But in 1895 the only lawyers in practice at Shanghai were British lawyers who were allowed, by courtesy, to present their clients' cases in their own language before all consular officers except the French. Of late years many of these officers have had legal training, and one could always get a case properly tried at any rate in the Danish or Norwegian

Consulates. In cases tried by the French Consul we were obliged, before the French lawyers arrived, to employ some intelligent French clerk to put forward a claim against a French citizen.

Civil or criminal proceedings against Chinese residents within the International Settlement Area had to be taken in a Court called the Mixed Court presided over by a Chinese Magistrate with whom sat a consular Assessor. In this court also we were allowed to use the English language, speeches being interpreted by our own interpreters to the Magistrate. Most of the business of the Mixed Court consisted in dealing with the crimes of a large city, the prosecutors being the Municipal Police. During the greater part of the present century the Council have employed a police legal assistant of their own and my firm has been relieved of much irksome labour, although its aid was occasionally sought in prosecutions of special importance. We were glad to be rid of the ordinary police work, but did not approve of the way in which the transfer was arranged. We had been put to a good deal of trouble in securing a remarkably brilliant young solicitor to attend to this department of our business and were shocked when he told us that, on the advice of one of the senior officials of the Council, he proposed to break his contract with us and join the Municipal Service as police legal assistant – as to his covenant not to practice apart from us we could do what we pleased. Of course we did nothing as we did not feel that the boy was really to blame, and it was not to our advantage to quarrel with our clients, the Council. But we thought that we had been scurvily treated.

Besides dealing with crime, the Mixed Court also adjudicated upon civil claims brought against Chinese residents either by their own countrymen or by foreigners. In the latter class of cases a consular Assessor of the plaintiff's nationality sat with the Magistrate. The Chinese are a litigious people and many of the smaller legal firms practically lived on the fees they received in civil cases between Chinese, and Chinese and rarely appeared in the Supreme Court. We had a good deal of this kind of work, so much, indeed, that we added to our staff a young Chinese who had been called to the English bar. He was a clever, hard-working, and trust-worthy man, and was much respected by the more reputable members of the native community, so that he never involved us in any shady business. After my first ten years I did not go to the Mixed Court except for very important clients. They only dealt with men of established reputation and some of them used to boast that they had never had a written contract but merely a note in their books of a transaction. But this state of things did not long outlast the Revolution of 1911. One instance will serve to illustrate the change. An old comprador with fifty years of service and the entire confidence of his employers, pretended that Chinese buyers were very slow in taking delivery of goods imported under contract. One day his firm were shocked by the receipt of a threat of proceedings for non-delivery, and was led to the discovery that its *godowns* (warehouses) were quite empty, the comprador having sold every bale of goods for his own benefit. The man admitted his offence and promptly committed suicide, leaving the firm to face an almost ruinous loss.

The British Bar consisted of about fifteen barristers or solicitors, grouped into five or six firms. Most of the important business houses retained either ourselves or the firm which is now Platt & Co (just as we have become Hansons) but which had many different names in the years following 1895. Drummond was mainly concerned with Chinese, including Chinese Government interests. H.S. Wilkinson (afterwards Sir Hiram, and Chief Justice) was Crown Advocate and had with him his son, who succeeded him in that office.

In our own firm Hanson attended to most of the conveyancing, while Dowdall handled the business of the Municipal Council and generally advised all important clients. They could not have had a better adviser. His opinions were always clear, concise, and definite and were expressed in admirable language; he took a great deal of trouble to ensure that they were correct. Dowdall had a horror of the elaborately itemised bills of some solicitors and always charged clients what he thought was a reasonable lump sum for work done. Under the head of "work" he did not include telephone attendances and the reading of letters. Although his charges were never excessive I think that he sometimes showed an insufficient appreciation of the feelings of clients. If a man objected to his bill he told him that he need not pay it and should take his business elsewhere in future. That was not quite fair, if a client objects to a bill he should be told that he can have it taxed. A man should not be threatened with a severance of relations merely because he stands on his rights. In Dowdall's case especially, I think a mistake was made because he habitually undercharged and must have been certain that his bill would be allowed by the Taxing Master. Matters, however, were not often pushed to extremes, for Dowdall's reputation for fairness stood so high that objecting clients generally ended by paying what he asked.

We were always on very intimate terms with Platt & Co. and their predecessors, and our friendly relations contributed in no small degree to the settlement of disputes without litigation or, where no litigation was likely, to agreement between parties on matters of difference. We also gave each other a good deal of business when retainers prevented one of us from acting for a person who had asked for assistance. We had far more to do with them than with any other lawyers. It is difficult to exaggerate the importance of the relations of mutual confidence between our two firms in regard to the saving of expense to clients. Naturally we were often engaged in conflict which nevertheless did not in the least impair our friendship.

I had no sooner settled into my place in Dowdall & Hanson's office than I had to handle an important conveyance in connection with the amalgamation of two Dock Companies, one registered and the other unregistered. Both were to transfer their properties to a new company to be registered under the Hongkong Companies' Ordinances to which also further property of various tenures belonging to a third party was to be made over. It was a very complicated affair but I put it through, I am glad to say, to Hanson's satisfaction. The property concerned was worth, I dare say, £1,000,000 sterling.

I was sent very often to the Mixed Court on behalf of a wrong-headed client who required my presence in his office so frequently that at last Dowdall took to hiring me out at so much an hour paid in advance. This client was a man known as "The Lawyers' friend," because at one time or other he employed every firm in the place to fight cases which he always lost for the reason that they never had any real substance. None of his claims were utterly absurd, but they rested upon such slight foundations as to be scarcely honest. We soon got tired of him and passed him on.

I also appeared before Arbitrators on a fire claim, and once or twice in the Supreme Court, but my first case of any importance did not come to me till early in 1896 when Dowdall asked me to defend a man whom he knew and who was accused of obtaining money by false pretences. He had really no chance of an acquittal for he had pleaded guilty before the Magistrate, though he withdrew that plea at the trial and I did what I could for him. He had in fact behaved very badly for, after obtaining an advance from the Russian Bank on goods which he represented (the prosecution said "falsely") to be his, he shipped the goods to England and drew against them for a sum which he appropriated and spent. It was not likely that so honest a judge as Hannen would strain any point in his favour and he was duly convicted on the only charge made against him (false pretences) and sentenced to eighteen months imprisonment, - a long sentence for Shanghai. But while I had no sympathy with my client, I think that he was wrongly convicted. Although I elicited in cross-examination from the Manager of the Bank that he was absent in Japan at the time when the pretence was said to have been made to him, the charge was never amended so that the accused could not properly have been found guilty. Moreover, I proved clearly that the goods did, in fact, belong to him; they were lying at his sole disposal in his own hired *godown* subject only to his obligation to pay his Chinese seller. But Hannen, being as I have said, very honest, brushed all this aside: and though I was not in the least sorry for the man, I do not think that as a judge he was justified in doing so. The criminal was well known in Shanghai society and it was thought that he greatly aggravated his offence by wearing a hat with the Country Club ribbon during his summer in gaol.

All claims against the Municipal council had to be brought before a tribunal called the Court of Consuls which consisted of three consuls nominated by the consular body. The Senior Consul of the day was a member of the Court, ex officio, and the British and U.S. Consuls General were usually members on account of the preponderant interest of their nationals in the community. The Court of Consuls was bound by no law or precedent and dealt with each case on its merits after the manner of Arbitrators. During my early years, the Council (an annually elected body) usually consisted of seven British subjects, one American and one German; it being recognized that although the number of British subjects entitled to the voting franchise would have made it possible for them to return an entirely British Council it was desirable, in the interests of peace, to associate subjects of other nations with the Government of the Settlement. In those days, the Court viewed with jealousy any extension of municipal authority and Dowdall's policy was to keep the Council out of Court if possible, there being always a risk that if a case was fought, a judgment might deprive them of some absolutely necessary power.

The Land Regulations (Shanghai's constitution) dated from the sixties, and as amendment required the consent of all the ministers of the Treaty Powers and of the Chinese Government, and was, therefore, practically impossible; they had to be a good deal strained to make them fit new conditions of life. It was always in the power of an indisposed Court to clog the wheels of the Municipal Machine by a too rigid construction of some antiquated Regulation. Dowdall, therefore, was nearly always in favour of compromise and, during the twenty or more years during which I was the Council's legal adviser, I was considerably influenced by his views. But we had to fight sometimes, and I am bound to say that the attitude of the Court became much more reasonable as years went on. It seemed, to put the matter shortly, to appreciate at last the fact that the Municipal government had not only to be carried on but to be carried on under the Regulations and, when it felt bound to decide against the Council, to base its decision on grounds other than a doubtful construction of a Land Regulation. But it was not easy to advise in any particular case as to what was likely to be the attitude of a Court which often included representatives of the smaller Powers whose interest in the well-being of the Settlement was not strong. I have known such a Court to give a sympathetic decision in favour of an employee's claim for wrongful dismissal on the grounds that the rules which the Council claimed that he had broken were not properly brought to his notice, although the Court had before it the plaintiff's copy of his agreement to which was annexed a copy of the rules. And I have known a Court of Consuls to hold that the taking of land for a garbage dump was not justified by a clause in the Land Regulations giving power to take land for "Public Purposes". Of course, the Court's decisions were not always so obviously open to criticism as these are, but I am quite safe in stating that it was seldom possible to be sure of winning even the best case.

Soon after I joined the firm, the Council appeared to be dissatisfied with Dowdall's court work on their behalf. I doubt if they had any good reason for their dissatisfaction. His last appearance for them in the Supreme Court had been in a case which he lost before

T.M. Thorp

Hannen through no fault of his, but which was easily won on appeal to the Privy Council. Anyhow, in the next Court of Consuls case that came on, the Council desired that I should appear for them. It was a case that had to be fought, but in which success was bound to depend on the sympathy of the Court. The question involved was whether the Council, which had acquired from a company the Electrical Plant which supplied the Settlement, was entitled to sell electrical fittings in competition with private traders. There was obviously a good deal to be said on both sides, but the Court was against me, with the result that a large stock of fittings intended to supply the public for years had to be sold in the open market at a very heavy loss and was, of course, bought by private concerns. The case might well have gone the other way, but it happened that the members of the Court disapproved of Municipal trading and felt no compunction in penalizing the community as a whole in the interests of a few firms.

During 1896 and 1897 I do not think that we had any very interesting work, though we were busy all the time. We had one case, I remember, for the Nanking Viceroy against a British firm which had sold him some remarkably bad rifles and charged him about double the price of good ones. Our expert told us that these old Austrian muzzleloaders, now converted into breechloaders, could not be fired by anyone without risk of his life. However, the case fizzled out on some technicality. The Viceroy, I think, found it impossible in view of his position to sign the submission to jurisdiction without which the British Court could not entertain claims by foreigners. And I recollect prosecuting an American citizen, who was one of the Li Hung Chang's hangers-on, for assaulting a journalist who had made rather strong comments on that Viceroy's shady entourage. The client was so pleased with the fine of $1 (gold) inflicted by the U.S. Consul General that he gave me, in addition to my fee, a roll of silk said to come from the Empress Dowager's private store (which still covers some of my furniture). But on the whole, as far as my memory serves me, these were uneventful years. We did, however, bring out in 1896 the first of many cotton mill companies that were registered under the Hongkong Ordinance. The mill belonged to Messrs. Jardine Matheson & Co. and the Memorandum and Articles had been drawn by one of their employees. Our instructions were that, as the man was very valuable and very sensitive, we should spare his feelings and make only such alterations in his draft as were positively required by law. This, as any lawyer will appreciate, was a difficult job and I think it was creditable to us that we were able to accomplish it at all. But we were never quite sure that we had put the

Company in a safe position and were relieved when, a few years later, new Articles were required and we were able to draw these in common form.

Dowdall was at home in 1896 and Hanson in 1897. At the beginning of 1898 the firm did me the honour of making me a partner, although I had still nearly a year to serve under my agreement and, what was more generous still, they allowed me to take a holiday of nine months at home, which after seven years of work abroad was very welcome. Walford, who had not been able to get away from Japan since I left him, was anxious that I should, if possible, take charge of his practice for two months on my way to England, so that he might make a trip to Honolulu. He offered the use of his house and servants and liberal payment for my work. I was glad to be able to fall in with his wishes, and we spent a very pleasant time in Yokohama, visiting old haunts, and seeing old friends. There was not much serious business coming forward, but the Japanese had lately required all foreign patents and trademarks to be registered as a condition of protection and Walford had a good deal to do in this connection. I carried on this work during his absence with the assistance of my old acquaintance, Okamura. During my visit to Japan, I had an amusing case before H.B.M. Consul-General at Yokohama sitting as Police Magistrate. Lowder was on the other side and was prosecuting a recently arrived Bank official for assault, he having, it was alleged, ejected his landlord with violence from his compound and cast him down a flight of steps. I believe that the accused had, in fact, done this or something like it, his excuse being that the man was trespassing, and so, in law, he was. But perhaps rather too much vigour had been displayed in connection with his exit. Very little damage, however, had been done and after a really enjoyable hearing which lasted two days the Consul-General inflicted a fine of yen 8 (16/-). The result looked like a moral victory, and so my client thought, for he overwhelmed me with expressions of gratitude and did not grudge me my fee of yen 100.

Most of our time at home had to be spent quietly in the houses of our relations, for my double change of courts had not left us much spare cash. But Dowdall had added to his other kindness by guaranteeing a sufficient Letter of Credit so that we were able to take full advantage of our leave. We returned to Shanghai before Christmas 1898.

Early in 1899 I appeared in what I may call my first "cause celebrée". A British Consul had died leaving a widow who claimed against an Insurance Company under a policy effected by her husband on his life. The Company were clients of another firm and I was brought into the case to conduct it, with their barrister assistance as my nominal leader. The defence was based on false representations and concealment of facts and the case proved to be a long and interesting one. It was a jury case and the widow had a good deal of public sympathy, the court being packed every day with her supporters. We were rather anxious about the result, but relied on Hannen's good sense and the very clear and definite evidence of the doctors who had in times past attended the deceased for acute disease of the heart, which had apparently escaped his memory when he offered himself for insurance. The company won their case and, I think, were fully justified in fighting it. When they had secured their verdict they acted with good judgment in paying a substantial sum to the plaintiff *ex gratia*. It is impossible not to feel some sympathy with a man who knows that he is a bad life and must leave his family destitute unless he can get himself insured as a good one: but Insurance Companies would soon have to go out of business unless they occasionally stood up for their rights. In this case, the Company came in for a good deal of undeserved criticism. In the course of the proceedings, a remarkably inept question was asked by Counsel for the plaintiff in re-examining a highly respectable medical witness who happened to be his father-in-law. "I suppose, doctor," he said, "that your connection with me has not influenced your evidence in any way?" I shall never forget the tone in which Hannen commented, "Really, Mr. - - !"

About this time, I had a case in the U.S. Court which left an unpleasant impression on my mind. The Marshal of the Court had taken some land into his name to hold in trust for a Chinese, natives of China not being able to hold land in the Settlement in their own names. He then mortgaged it for his own benefit and I was claiming that he should redeem the mortgage and transfer the property to a nominee of my client. The Consul-General granted me the relief which I asked for, but ordered the plaintiff to pay the costs and absolutely refused to allow me to make any reference to the fraudulent mortgage. But what disgusted me was that a missionary, one of the two assessors, as he came into Court, jovially slapped the defendant on the shoulder and addressed him by a familiar nick-name, although he knew as a fact that this scoundrel was guilty of conduct which was bound to affect the reputation of all foreigners who were in the habit of acting as trustees for Chinese. In such matters there was always a period between the issue of a consular title deed to a foreign registered owner and the delivery of it to the native beneficial owner, when the person named in the deed could deal with the land as his own by selling or mortgaging it. The development of Shanghai has been to a large extent due to the investment of Chinese capital in land and buildings, such investment being based upon complete confidence in the probity of the foreigners concerned, and even an isolated instance of dishonesty such as that of this defendant was calculated to impair that feeling. By far the greater part of the land held for Chinese is registered in British names, a fact which clearly indicates the Chinese estimate of our national character. But it is difficult for Chinese to distinguish accurately between British and Americans or to realize that no inference affecting the honesty of British trustees could fairly be drawn from the fraud of an important officer of the U.S. Court.

In 1901, the firm suffered a very serious loss through the death of Dowdall, who was drowned when the American liner, "City of Rio", sank outside the Golden Gates of San Francisco. In consequence of his death the whole business became the property of Hanson and myself. But the original partnership agreement between Dowdall and Hanson, the terms of which I had accepted, provided for very burdensome payments to Dowdall's widow and Hanson had to take a strong line with the executors before he could bring them to any reasonable arrangement. We did not object to paying a specified sum for five years out of the profits of our law department, but we did not consider it fair that we should hand over Dowdall's share of our Land Agency profits as long as we continued to carry on such business. This provision prevented us from offering reasonable terms to a new partner, so we agreed that rather than comply with it we would give up Land Agency altogether and sell the goodwill to one of our competitors. Faced with this decision, the executors showed their good sense by accepting a lump sum of, I think, £4,000, and releasing us from the burden of the clause. When Hanson and I came to draw up a new agreement we were led by this experience to adopt the simplest conditions possible, namely that on the death or retirement of a partner the business should belong to the surviving or continuing partners, who had only to pay out whatever their late colleague had paid for his interest. When I became a partner, the rule was that nothing was paid for share in the law business but a newcomer paid his proportion of the amount originally spent in acquiring the Land Agency. But after Dowdall's death there had to be added to this amount whatever we had paid to his widow, and the obligations of a new partner were further increased when Hanson required a compensation for his sudden retirement in 1908, on the occasion of his marriage.

Hanson and I found that we had more work than we could cope with, so we engaged a young solicitor at home in 1904. He is now the senior partner in the firm.

The six months which followed Dowdall's death were very busy ones for me, as Hanson went to California to assist the widow and bring her husband's body to

Shanghai for burial. He was absent from March to September and I am proud to be able to say that our earnings did not drop during this period. But my old clerk and I had a strenuous time, working from 8.30 a.m. to 7.30 p.m. every day, and I also had to take papers home whenever I had a case in Court. The old man attended to the Land Agency, fair-copied letters, and engrossed deeds and wills. We had no typists or stenographers in those days. I found that I saved a great deal of time by always going to the Shanghai Club between twelve and one and staying there to lunch, for I had an opportunity of talking to clients or other lawyers and of thus avoiding much correspondence. At the end of my six months I felt very well indeed, although I had had little of the hard exercise which I had always considered necessary to health in summer. After that experience, I practically abandoned my old habits and indulged in no violent exertions during the hot weather. Many men, I am sure, made themselves ill by playing too much cricket and tennis with the shade temperature at 95°. But the carrying on single-handed of a business, which had fully occupied three people, had really been too much for me and one night, when I was pouring out a drink before going to bed, I spoke to my wife in gibberish, and was unable to frame a single intelligible sentence. I knew quite well what I wanted to say, and was much interested in my symptoms, so I wanted my wife to take down my remarks, but as she was reduced nearly to tears I could not urge her to do so. Next morning I had entirely recovered and I have never had the slightest return of aphasia. My doctor at once sent me off for a shooting trip, which no doubt completed my cure. He said that overwork was the cause of my irregular behaviour, although I myself was quite unconscious of any ill effects except that, for half an hour, I had been unable to control my speech. The broad difference between practice at home and in the Far East is that we exiles usually worked under much less strain and were seldom hustled, and I suppose that I was affected by the sudden change to something like home conditions.

Hannen most unfortunately died at the end of the century, just as he was looking forward to his retirement. He had more of the "judicial instinct" than any other judge (excepting Fielding Clark) before whom I have practised. He was impartial, courteous and patient, very dignified, and quite a good enough lawyer for his position. After he had been appointed Chief Justice he withdrew himself almost entirely from general society, although he welcomed his intimate friends in his own home. Shanghai is, after all, comparatively a small place, and by avoiding the company of possible litigants he, no doubt, spared himself from a good deal of embarrassment. At the same time, I must say that I have known judges who were quite as impartial, but who were not so sensitive. But in such matters every man is surely entitled to regulate his conduct as he thinks fit. Hannen was succeeded by Wilkinson who from being Crown Advocate had become Judge of H.B.M. Court for Japan and sat as such during the last years of the Court's existence. He was a judge of a different type, being chiefly remarkable for an indifference to the conflicting views of litigants which was so complete as almost to resemble impartiality, although his attitude was really due to a passionate desire to avoid being reversed by the Privy Council. If a plaintiff or defendant was able to present a few facts which could be found in his favour and were sufficient to bring him within the protection of a safe line of cases, he was certain to succeed. He always reserved his judgments and delivered very lengthy ones. Wilkinson was a rigid formalist and did much to tighten up the practice of the Court which had become rather slack. This judge had one peculiarity which was most embarrassing to Counsel, namely that he often chose to base his decisions on authorities discovered by himself rather than on those which were brought to his notice in Court. So the victor got no credit for his victory and the loser complained that he had had no opportunity of distinguishing his case from the case or cases which the

Chief Justice was prepared to follow. Although he lacked some judicial qualities, he was clever and well-read.

A great contrast to Sir Hiram Wilkinson was Mr. (now Sir Frederick) Bourne, who, during a great part of the former's tenure of office, held the post of Assistant Judge and acted as Chief Justice when Wilkinson was on leave. Bourne was only called to the Bar after he had risen fairly high in the Consular service and, while reading for his call, had conceived a great admiration for Roman and a great contempt for English law. Unfortunately for his reputation it was English law which it was his duty to administer. He was an able and very fair-minded man and a good criminal judge, but his intolerance of precedent, and his conviction that any civil case could be decided by common sense, made it extraordinarily difficult for lawyers to advise their clients on points of law. The commercial community took the only course open to it and entirely deserted the Court, referring all disputes to legal arbitrators. Our firm suffered considerable inconvenience from the fact that Hanson's services were much in request as Arbitrator and that, while his fee was a very small compensation for his expenditure of time and trouble, the members of our firm could not appear before him as counsel and our receipts from law business suffered a serious diminution. Neither lawyers nor the public dared to contemplate the possible promotion of

T.M. Thorp

Bourne on the retirement of the Chief Justice, but as it turned out, a successor was brought in from outside. I have heard Bourne tell a jury in a libel case, in which the libel complained of did not mention the Plaintiff by name or accuse him of definite misconduct, that they should disregard the innuendo as irrelevant, and consider the words of the libel in the light of common sense. If newspaper reports are to be believed (and I think this one was accurate) he once left the Court, after a case had been argued before him for some days, with the observation, "this is a very complicated matter and should never have been brought into Court at all. The parties had better settle it among themselves", and he refused any further hearing. One of Bourne's chief defects was that, having no experience of practice, he did not in the least understand the relations between the Bar and the public, and was too apt to think that bad cases would never come to court unless counsel had previously advised that they were good ones. He was a man of fine presence and might have been a good all round judge if he had ever realized that a judge's duty often compelled him to put aside his own feelings. He once went so far as to give judgment against an insurance company which pleaded, in defence to a claim, that the plaintiff had violated the conditions of the policy, on the ground that a Chinese could not be expected to understand the terms of an English contract. His sympathy with the claimant blinded him to the fact that there could be no hardship in holding that a man who, on his own showing, understood the provision of the policy which was in his favour, namely the Company's promise to pay, must be presumed to know that this promise was conditional and what the conditions were: otherwise there was no contract.

My success in defending an insurance company in 1899 led to our being connected with the formation of the China Mutual Life Insurance Company Limited, whose principal business was intended to be the insurance of Chinese lives. This Company prospered greatly owing to the ability and energy of its founder and to very exceptional luck in the matter of claims during its early years. Before long it ran the Sun Life of Canada out of the field, and its founder lived long enough to see the last named company (just the other day) taking over the great business which he had built up on terms satisfactory to his shareholders. The insurance of Chinese lives is a very difficult business to start, for it is essential to acquire, as soon as possible, a reputation for prompt settlement of claims. To secure this a number of claims must be paid without too close examination, while on the other hand gross fraud must from time to time be exposed by way of example. We fought very few cases for the China Mutual

Life Insurance Company, but those which we fought we won. In one case which I remember, the insured was recognised in a tea-shop some months after payment of a claim based on his alleged death. In another, which we contested on the ground of concealment of ill health, we were able to produce a letter written by the deceased which ran more or less as follows: "My dear friend, As you know I have long been a sick man and I am not likely to live for many months; your health – you have often told me – is as bad as mine. But I have lately insured my life with a generous company, The China Mutual, and I strongly advise you to follow my example. This Company is not too particular and you can easily arrange for your examination to be made by a doctor who will know well enough how to fill up the Company's forms in a satisfactory manner." The insured was a dealer in a small way but when he was introduced to the Company's agent he was dressed in expensive robes and was occupying a house in a good quarter which had been lent by a complaisant acquaintance – no doubt on terms. This Company gave us a great deal of conveyancing business as a large part of its funds was invested in Shanghai on mortgages of property owned by Chinese.

A question of murder was involved in a curious way in a case in which I appeared before Bourne. The master of a coasting steamer was found dead in his bunk with a discharged rifle lying beside him and he was succeeded in command of the ship by his chief officer. A friend of the dead man was convinced that the chief officer had murdered his superior with a view to stepping into his shoes, and he allowed his opinion, which I am sure was sincere, to carry him to strange lengths. For example, he invited reporters to a gruesome reconstruction of what he called the crime, a leg of mutton taking the place of the dead captain's head in his bunk and intercepting a rifle bullet. He also caused handbills to be printed with the words, "Why do you travel on a ship commanded by a murderer?", and placed them in the cabins of the passengers. The Company which owned the steamer was much concerned about these happenings and at last told the new master that he must put an end to them or resign his command. It seemed probable that his enemy had conceived the insane idea that if he could force him to take proceedings for libel he would be able to have the question of his guilt investigated in a civil suit. The harassed man came to me for advice as to what steps he could take and asked me whether I did not think that a little beating up might have a good effect. I told him that he must on no account allow himself to be forced into a libel action, but that, if he took the law into his own hands, he would certainly be charged with assault. He left my chambers and returned in a quarter of an hour to say that he had administered a severe thrashing. A summons for assault naturally followed and was heard by Bourne sitting as Police Magistrate. I was able to bring out in cross-examination of the complainant all the details of his conduct which had led my client to commit a breach of the peace, and Bourne, with the comment that such provocation was more than human nature could endure, bound both parties over, my client, of course, having pleaded guilty. The persecution ceased at once and there was no longer any question of a libel suit. My client seemed to me to be a sensible fellow, and therefore I always doubted whether he had really murdered his shipmate, there being so many easier and safer ways of getting command of a ship.

On another occasion, I appeared before Bourne, this time also sitting to take evidence on commission, in a case in which a Manchester firm was being sued in that city by a Shanghai merchant - an American - for damages in respect of the defective quality of goods shipped by them. The claim was for £8,000 and the commission was taken out by the Defendants who instructed me to call the Plaintiff and see what I could get from him in the way of evidence to support their case. I proceeded to do so, and things went well from the start, for the Plaintiff's answers were so unsatisfactory that Bourne soon allowed me to treat him as a hostile witness and to cross-examine him. But the end came much more quickly than I had expected. I had requested the man to produce, after the luncheon interval, certain receipts signed by Chinese for allowances, which he said that he had made to them on account of defective cargo and he promised to do so. But before we got to business again the American lawyer who was representing the plaintiff invited me to a private interview, when he told me that his client had just informed him that during the interval he had burned the receipts. He did not feel inclined, he said, to go on with the case and would consent to judgment for the Defendants with costs limited to the sum deposited as security in Manchester, if we would pay £250. This proposal was cabled to my clients who accepted gracefully, and when we next appeared before Bourne we surprised him by asking him to attest as judge a formal consent to judgment for production to the Manchester Court. My clients were extremely grateful, but did not pay my costs for four years and only then under rather sharp pressure from my London agents. Some clients are like that.

A case of mine in Hongkong interested the community one very hot summer. It was an "ice" case. My clients had sold an ice plant guaranteed to make ice "as good as that of the Hongkong Ice Company," and the purchasers said that it did not come up to the guarantee. They claimed the right to return the plant and to recover heavy damages for loss of profit. Piggott allowed the first part of their claim, but not the second which was the substantial part. The case turned on the meaning of the words "as good as". My client's plant produced ice, which was beautiful and sparkling and was, therefore, to that extent, good: but it was not too long lasting. The ice of the Hongkong Ice Company was dull and ugly, but solid, and, in a test for endurance, gained several points against its more attractive rival. The meaning of "goodness", therefore, seemed to depend on what you wanted the ice for - your dinner table or your icebox. Judge and Counsel inspected both brands of ice *in situ* and it was obvious that while the huge grey slabs exhibited by the Hongkong Ice Company had no aesthetic qualities at all, the neat clear blocks produced by my clients' plant were extremely pleasing to the eye. In fact, the chief Justice admitted in his judgment that he much preferred them, and my own opinion is that they were quite "good" enough to compete on even terms with the Company's ice. But, as it happened, the Plaintiffs were not in a position to compete, as they were insolvent and had only taken proceedings with the object of getting rid of a plant which they were not able to use. The result of the endurance test won them their first point and their insolvency no doubt contributed to the rejection of their claim for damages. The case, perhaps, helped to keep the public cool, as they talked of nothing else for weeks.

A Barrister in the Far East

In 1901 or 1902 I was brought in by another firm to conduct a libel suit against a man who had accused their client - a newspaper correspondent - of sending home the "Peking Massacre" telegrams which caused so much pain to relations and friends of those who were shut up in the beleaguered area, and even led to arrangements being made for a memorial service at St. Paul's. I was able to produce all the originals of the telegrams sent by the client, and comparison of these cabled messages with the reports published by the London newspapers for which he acted as correspondent threw a very unpleasant light on the methods of the sensation-mongering press. What the plaintiff, who had maintained very close touch with the best informed circles in Shanghai, had telegraphed were concise and accurate reports of official opinion as to the situation, none of his messages going so far as to say that the Legations had fallen. What the papers had published were lurid and detailed accounts of the horrible butchery which ensued after the Legations fell. The plaintiff got his verdict, but I nearly deprived him of it by pressing a lying witness too hard about some matter of prejudice. A juryman said to me afterwards: "I knew all about that business and I made up my mind that if you pressed those questions I would find for the defendant. But then I thought that though your client was a blackguard he could hardly be such a blackguard as to send those reports, so I gave him his verdict." I may perhaps be assumed to have learnt a lesson, for I practised afterwards for many years and did not make a similar blunder. I admit that it was a bad one, only explained but not excused by my desire to discredit as much as possible a witness whom I knew to be perjured. In this case I had Drummond against me and he had as his junior a barrister who now occupies a very high position at the English bar. After I had examined the plaintiff the case looked pretty "healthy", but the man's reputation was not good and I feared Drummond's cross-examination. He began this late one afternoon, but never appeared in the case again. Illness was the excuse which he put forward, but my impression is that he felt himself beaten by the facts and ran away. He left his junior in the position of having, quite unexpectedly, to cross-examine the plaintiff, on whose evidence the result largely depended, and to conduct the whole case for the defence. I thought that he did his duty admirably under very trying circumstances.

In the autumn of 1902, I was called to Tientsin to advise certain British shareholders in a company called the Chinese Engineering and Mining Company Limited, who were not satisfied with the manner in which the Company was controlled from London. They considered that, as in the case of the Shanghai Waterworks Company

Limited, (also a London Company), the management should consist of a local Board and a London Committee and, as I was going home in 1903, they wanted me to see what I could do towards furthering their wishes. During the course of my visit, I was approached on behalf of Chang Yen Mao, a Chinese official who had been the active agent in the transfer to the Mining Company of the mine which it was working. He also had a grievance against the Company on the ground that although at the time of the transfer he had stipulated for a considerable amount of Chinese participation in the management of the Company's affairs, Chinese rights in this connection had been entirely ignored. He instructed me to place the matter in the hands of solicitors and request them to press the Company to carry out the original arrangement; and he furnished me with ample funds for payment of expenses. But on no account was there to be litigation.

When I returned to Shanghai, I consulted the senior partner of the firm, which from that time onward acted as our London agents. He happened to be visiting Shanghai and, on his advice, I wrote to a firm of high standing with which we had had some previous dealings and asked them to handle the matter. In my letter I gave a very minute and detailed description of the situation, as I understood it, and especially of certain peculiar incidents connected with the promotion of the Mining

Company. It may be supposed that when I received a cable, "Regret acting for promoter," I was rather upset, for I had placed my opponents in possession of my whole case and, in particular, had given them warning as to the direction from which the attack was likely to come. I again had recourse to my friend, and he gave me the name of another first-class firm, who, however, were strangers to me. This firm agreed to get my letter out of the hands into which it had unluckily fallen, and to act on my instructions. Before I got home, I received the good news that the Directors had promised a great deal of what was required. It was therefore very disappointing to learn on my arrival that the situation was entirely changed and that the Directors refused to make any concession.

The explanation of the Directors' behaviour was remarkable. Shortly after I left China the Chinese Government, which had never ceased to protest through diplomatic channels against the transfer of the mine, began to make things very unpleasant for Chang Yen Mao, who was accused of having made over to foreigners property in which the Government had a large interest, and was told that he must either put matters right or forfeit his life. He had preferred the former alternative and had obtained leave to go to England and take legal proceedings. As a preliminary step he had cabled instructions to Messrs. Hollams to issue a writ against the promoter and the company, and had forwarded to them the copy of my letter which I had supplied to him as my client. When the writ came out the Directors, of course, drew in their horns. All this had happened without notice to me, but I regarded it as, in effect, a termination of my authority and accordingly paid my solicitors' charges and apologised for having given them unnecessary trouble. They had really done remarkably well and they let me off very lightly in the matter of costs. As I mentioned above, I had received a very substantial sum against the expenses of negotiating with the Board and it is characteristic of the Chinese attitude in matters of this kind that I had the greatest difficulty in repaying the balance remaining in my hands after I had deducted my own charges and all disbursements including my solicitors' costs. It was only after years of correspondence that I succeeded in obtaining authority to hand the money over to Chang Yen Mao's nominee. Apparently, Chang was merely irritated by my insistence on keeping open an account which he considered closed.

Chang Yen Mao's action excited a good deal of interest in England and the judgment, more or less in his favour, was the subject of a leader in the Times. It was suggested by Messrs. Hollams that perhaps my shareholder clients might be inclined to co-operate in some way with Chang, but after an interview with Mr. Hawkesley I was satisfied that it would be impossible for them to do so. What they desired was control in China, not control by Chinese. Chang Yen Mao certainly obtained a qualified success and had the full sympathy of the Court, but it was impossible to grant him all that he claimed without violating the provisions of the Companies Act. At any rate he saved his life. I was to hear a great deal more about the Chinese Engineering and Mining Company some years later, so I can pass away from it now.

In connection with Sir Hiram Wilkinson I must mention a case which I had before him during the Boxer outbreak. I was defending a Municipal policeman charged with unlawfully wounding a German soldier. Two drunken privates had been arrested on the complaint of a Chinese barber whose customers they were trying to shave. They were very violent when taken to the station and one of them eventually got away and had a fierce struggle in the veranda with the constable who was trying to prevent his escape. It was dark at the time, and, when the constable called out, "Take care! He has drawn his bayonet," the accused took a revolver from a drawer and fired a shot into the open air through the entrance door, with the object, he said, of terrifying the German. Unluckily the man had just broken loose and received the shot through his body; the same bullet also wounded a Chinese on the other side of the compound.

It was, I believe, a well-intentioned but rather reckless shot; and when the wounded man had recovered, the German military authorities insisted on a prosecution. They might well have dropped a matter so discreditable to their troops. I had no expectation of getting my client off scot-free, for it was generally felt that he had lost his head. Wilkinson was dead against him all through, and went so far as to tell the jury that, if the soldier had died, the offence would have been murder! This was more than they could stand, so they brought in a verdict of "not guilty", being afraid of what the Chief Justice might do if they gave him a chance. If it was not a correct verdict, the responsibility did not lie with the jury.

Another case, which I had before this judge, illustrates rather well the inconveniences which may result from extraterritoriality. A British and a German steamer were in collision and the British owners sued in the German Court, whose judgment was to the effect that the collision was solely due to the fault of the British ship. The owners of the German ship then instructed me to sue for their damage in H.B.M. Supreme Court, where I wished to rely on the finding of the German Admiralty Court as conclusive. Wilkinson, however, ruled that the German Court had no jurisdiction to make such a finding and that the evidence must be gone into afresh. Although the British owners had submitted to the foreign court's jurisdiction, I cannot say positively that the ruling was wrong. It was, however, very inconvenient and the more so that the point had not been raised by the pleadings. But our damages were not serious, and my German clients agreed with me that we should abandon proceedings.

Just before Sir Hiram Wilkinson's retirement I had a sharp brush with him regarding his treatment of a client. I was acting for a ship-broker who claimed commission for charter of a ship, which commission, he said, was wrongfully detained by the defendants. It was a jury case and before it had been long in progress Wilkinson, as usual, took a new point and put it to the jury that the evidence they had already heard, viewed in the light of his new discovery, probably satisfied them that the plaintiff had no case. The jury replied promptly that they were not satisfied, so the action went on to a conclusion. Wilkinson, instead of asking the jury to find for plaintiff or defendant (in which case as I afterwards learned they would have found for the plaintiff) asked them certain questions, which did not raise the point already referred to them, and adjourned the case for legal argument as to the effect of their answers. As it was not included in the jury's answers this point was not dealt with in argument by counsel on either side. It was, however, founded on by Wilkinson in his judgment as establishing the defendant's case, and he gave him judgment <u>with costs</u>. I did not think that this was fair in the circumstances, and I said so. The Chief Justice assured me that this was the first occasion on which he had ever been accused of doing a wilful injustice and added that he would decline to hear me until I had apologised. As I had nothing to apologise for I did not accept the suggestion: but later on, it was pointed out to me that this had been Wilkinson's last case, and that he was much upset about the matter, having known me for so long. I was pressed to reconsider my attitude and accordingly I wrote that I was sorry if anything that I had said had been interpreted as a reflection upon the manner in which he had discharged his judicial duties. This proved to be sufficient and when the Chief Justice took leave of the Bar he expressed his satisfaction at having received a letter from me which completely restored the old friendly relations. I am glad that I forced myself to write, for I had only a professional and not a personal grievance, and I should have been sorry to let the Chief Justice retire with the feeling that he had left ill will behind him. Moreover, it is always easier to apologise when you are in the right than when you are in the wrong.

Wilkinson (our last Chief Justice) retired in 1905 and was succeeded by de Sausmarez, the Chief Judge in Constantinople who was knighted very soon after his arrival. This change brought about the return of Sir Hiram Wilkinson's son, the Crown Advocate, who had been obliged to give up his practice in Shanghai on his father's appointment as Chief Justice. The Government was sympathetic and appointed him Commissioner to adjudicate on British claims for damages sustained through the Boxer rising and afterwards made him acting Judge in Siam. Not satisfied with this generosity the Foreign Office later on offered him the judgeship, which he declined. But he retained his post as Crown Advocate during his four years of absence, Platt or I acting for him all the time. At first we adhered to the usual private arrangement under which we received half his salary but, when his absence had extended far beyond the period of an ordinary leave, we took the matter up with the Foreign Office and after the first year were paid the full salary of £600 (£500 plus £100 for Wei-hai-wei). The criminal work was not heavy, though we had more than an average number of prosecutions: but the task of advising H.M. Minister took up a lot of time. A good deal of research was required before a definite opinion could be expressed on the question whether the Minister should approve new Harbour Rules for Amoy or an Amendment of the Chinkiang Land Regulations. I consider that we fully earned our salaries.

Sir Havilland de Sausmarez was a good lawyer and had a quick mind, so that it was always a pleasure to argue a point of law before him. He was perhaps a little apt to rush to conclusions of fact as the following may serve to show. I prosecuted before him a man accused of shooting to death a person whom he found under compromising circumstances, in the company of a woman of very low character whom he described as his fiancée. His excuse was that he shot in self-defence and, giving evidence on his own behalf, he described in detail something like a Cumberland wrestling match in which his opponent's tactics compelled him to fire repeated shots at him. Our doctor's evidence, however, knocked this story on the head, as it was clear that after the first shot the victim could have stirred neither hand nor foot. Sir Havilland took no notice of this histrionic performance, but directed the jury that, if they liked to do so, they might find the accused guilty of manslaughter on the ground of irresistible provocation. "She was," he said, "no doubt 'a flighty girl'," "but English law excuses to some extent a man who discovers his wife or fiancée in the embrace of a stranger." I don't know where he got his law from, but he certainly was much too hasty in his judgment about the girl: for he stopped me from leading evidence as to her character, which was unspeakably bad. She had merely accompanied the dead man to his house in the ordinary exercise of her profession. The jury were only too glad to follow the Chief Judge's direction by bringing in a verdict of manslaughter and the accused received a sentence of eighteen months imprisonment for a most brutal and unjustifiable murder.

The most important part of my work was done during de Sausmarez' occupation of the Bench for he stayed with us for fifteen years. Business moved briskly during his regime, as litigants were always willing to submit their disputes to his decision. I think that they got on the whole very good judgments. He was not tolerant of incapacity, and during his time we did not see much in the Supreme Court of those lawyers whose ordinary field of work was the Mixed Court, where platitudes and personalities were quite in order and formed the staple of discourse. After his retirement, these people established themselves firmly in the Court, the atmosphere of which was entirely changed.

A Danish member of the Shanghai Club provoked the Committee by constantly describing in correspondence certain members, whose place of origin was Bagdad, as "camel drivers". They or their forebears had very possibly been engaged in this or some other humble occupation but, for the moment, he and they were members of the same club, and the Committee thought that the descendent of Vikings had behaved in an unbecoming manner. So they called a general meeting, which expelled him, and he sued in H.B.M. Supreme Court for restitution of his membership, the Club being registered as a Company under the Hongkong Ordinance. I defended, and had some trouble with the Plaintiff who was cunning if not clever, and deaf enough to hear what he wanted to hear, but nothing else. He was particularly deaf to cross-examination. For a long time he refused to hear or answer a question of mine as to why he was so anxious to get back to a club of "camel-drivers". At last he admitted that he heard, but assured me that he could not possibly answer - in private, perhaps, but certainly not in Court. Finally, with much affectation of modesty, he said that his reason for seeking to be reinstated as a member was that he wished to use the Club lavatories. This answer, and what went before, finished his case with de Sausmarez, if he had any. But I don't think that he ever had any chance of success, as he relied entirely on technical breaches of the rules relating to expulsion which, as the evidence showed, had never been committed.

In 1908 I appeared for the North China Daily News, the leading British newspaper in the Far East, in an action for libel brought by two barrister partners. A paragraph published in the newspaper had suggested that the conduct of these gentlemen had been unprofessional, and called for some action on the part of the Bar Committee. The Editor showed me the paragraph on the evening before publication and

T.M. Thorp

I passed it as a harmless, if one-sided, statement of facts; but to my horror it appeared next day under the heading of, "A case for the Bar Committee." As the libel could not be disputed, I tried hard to get an apology accepted: but the plaintiffs were "out for blood" and insisted on going to Court, where they fought the case with such bitterness that they very nearly lost it. Eventually the jury pooled their votes which ranged from nothing at all to [T]ls. 50,000 and gave them $5,000 (Mex.) each. This, I think, was a very fair verdict, not as representing special damages, for there was none, but as a penalty. The men had behaved badly in pushing themselves into a dispute, which was in course of settlement without legal assistance; but it would have been difficult to prove that they had done anything liable to censure even by a body possessing disciplinary powers. The Shanghai Bar Committee had none. I found my position as counsel for the newspaper very embarrassing, as my only chance of saving my clients from having to make substantial amends involved the introduction, in cross-examination, of matters of prejudice, which might just as well have increased as mitigated damages. My clients thought that I should have shown more energy in counter-attack, but, while I understood their views, I did not agree with them. In their next libel case the newspaper engaged other counsel and had to pay proportionately greater damages for a much less serious, because much less wanton, libel.

A Barrister in the Far East

In 1909, a new phase of my career began, for I was briefed to go "special" to Hongkong. It appeared that the Chief Justice there (the late Sir Francis Piggott) was making litigation almost impossible for the business community through his invariable preference for the arguments of one particular counsel. Things came to such a pass that the recognised leader of the Bar had to withdraw to London and practice before the Privy Council until Piggott's retirement. Accordingly, I was invited to go down and try to re-establish normal conditions. I was to be led (nominally) by a local "silk", but I was to conduct the proceedings and, if possible, to get the Chief Justice out of his groove. We had a sound case and my leader had got it up very thoroughly. Piggott gave me a good hearing and there were moments when we dared to think that we had won: but the Chief Justice was not to be so easily moved from his established practice. He went astray in his law but made his position secure by finding against us, on very flimsy evidence, a few facts essential to our success on appeal to the Privy Council. But the solicitors were pleased to have discovered someone who was at least able to secure the attention of the Court, and I received two or three briefs in cases to be heard in the next year. These, however, I had to return for a reason which will presently appear.

Before I went to Hongkong, I consulted Drummond, the only other barrister who went "special" in my time, for I had been offered a lump sum and I did not wish to undersell other members of our Bar. He told me that he would not himself have accepted such terms but advised me not to haggle about fees as it was to be my first visit. I must not omit to mention the kind reception, which was given to me by the members of the Hongkong Bar, in spite of the fact that I was trespassing on their preserves. I had, it is true, been a member of the Colonial Bar since 1895 and was, with the exception of Pollock, the senior member; but the barristers practising in Hongkong might have complained with reason of competition by one whom they knew to be associated with solicitors. However, neither then nor in later years, did they allow me to feel that I was regarded as an unwelcome intruder; and I have always thought that in this matter they showed great generosity.

I thoroughly enjoyed my sea trips (three days each way) and the fine summer weather of Hongkong. Big cases were usually held over until July or August, the earlier months of the year being damp and goffy, and most people (including members of the legal profession) preferring to take their holidays then in Japan or British Columbia, and to stay away until the weather became settled. It was a strange experience to come from Shanghai, quite deserted by women and children from mid-July to the end of September, and find a brisk social life going on so many degrees further South.

In 1910, I became concerned in an unusual piece of business, which took me away from my ordinary practice for a whole year. I received instructions from certain Chinese in Tientsin to proceed at once to that port in connection with important matters relating to the Chinese Engineering and Mining Company Limited. As the river approach to Tientsin was frozen, I had to land at Chingwantao, a port which is kept open all the year round by ice-breakers from the steamers of the Mining Company. From Chingwantao I travelled by rail to Tientsin and was met by Kingsley on behalf of my Chinese clients. Kingsley had been manager of the mine taken over by the Company at the time of the transfer by Chang Yen Mao. In his earlier years, he was a harbour master in the service of the Chinese Maritime Customs and earned the respect of all the Commissioners under whom he worked. After the transfer of the mine he became the adviser in financial and other matters of Chang Yen Mao and many important Chinese, by whom he was implicitly trusted. He thoroughly deserved their confidence; for a more honest and sensible man never lived. When he welcomed me in Tientsin, he had just been recalled from Vancouver where he had settled on his retirement from China a few years before. I had met Kingsley in the office of Messrs. Hollams in 1903, for he had accompanied Chang Yen Mao to England and took charge of all arrangements for his party. He explained the situation to me. Chinese business interests had been putting some pressure on the Viceroy of Chihli to recover the ownership of the mine by repurchase, and public meetings had passed rather violent resolutions. The Viceroy had obtained from the Chinese Government the promise of an issue of Government Bonds to an amount sufficient to cover the expense of repurchase. I had been invited to come North to advise as to how to proceed.

We had a great many meetings and much discussion, usually in the Li Hung Chang Memorial Temple and between the hours of 5.30 and 9.30 p.m. Neither the time nor the place selected for our conferences was very agreeable to me as I was never able to dine until 10.30 and the Temple (in February) was bitterly cold. The Chinese were most courteous and intelligent men, their chief spokesman being a Mr. Chow, who was managing director of a Chinese concern called the Lanchow Mining Company, whose immense coalfields adjoined the property of the Chinese Engineering and Mining Company Limited. After two or three weeks it was settled that I should go home with a P/A from the Viceroy and endeavour to negotiate the purchase at a price round about £1,500,000. I was instructed to act independently of the Chinese Legation if the Foreign Office would consent to receive me, and I was to do my best to enlist the sympathy of the British Government and particularly of Sir Edward Grey, the Secretary for Foreign Affairs. It was desired that I should express in the proper quarter, the hope of the Chinese Government that their old grievance regarding the transfer of the mine might be wiped out by the acceptance on the part of the British Company of reasonable conditions of sale.

In undertaking this mission no one, I think, will say that I underestimated my own capacity. My considered opinion is that in one respect at least I erred on the other side; for I was confident that I should be able to induce the Foreign Office to give me some active assistance, which, as it turned out, was steadily refused. Otherwise, all that I had to do was to make an offer, receive the Mining Company's reply and pass it on. Every further step had to be taken in accordance with specific instructions and all my doings had to be reported in detail either by cable or in writing.

As to remuneration, I had no cause to complain. I had expected that a fee would be suggested for my consideration, but I was directed through Kingsley to estimate a sum sufficient to cover my charges and expenses. I was giving up my practice for a whole year and I would also have to return my Hongkong briefs, so, with Kingsley's approval, I proposed £5,000 and £2,000 and my figures were accepted without demur. The

Chinese are in the habit of dealing generously with those in whom they place confidence and I was trusted because of Kingsley's support, for I was almost a stranger: my clients of their own accord paid me £3,500 in advance and placed a like sum on fixed deposit in my name with the Hongkong and Shanghai Bank for one year, only stipulating that they should receive the interest. By treating me in this way they, at any rate, made it certain that I should not spare myself in their service.

The Chinese were anxious that Kingsley should accompany me, and after many refusals he agreed to do so. I liked him very much and was glad to have his company throughout the negotiations, in which, however, he took no active part. He was fully acquainted with all particulars relating to the original transfer and his assistance was also invaluable in the coding and decoding of the long telegrams, which passed to and fro almost daily. We had a bad code to work on (the A.B.C.) and the drafting of an intelligible message often took us three or four hours.

When we reached London via Siberia early in April we called as a matter of courtesy on the Chinese Minister, Lord Li, who gave us a most civil reception. I had known him before as an old client of my firm. Then we visited the solicitors who had acted for me in 1903 and placed the matter in their experienced hands. Soon a letter to the Mining Company was drafted, printed, and despatched and I was in a position to call at the Foreign Office. There I saw the gentleman in charge of Chinese Affairs. He had heard all about me already from Peking, as I had thought it advisable to let H.M. Chargé d'Affairs know about the work which I had in hand: and the Legal Adviser had, on my request, drawn his attention to the fact that I had acted as Crown Advocate for two years on the instructions of the Secretary of State for Foreign Affairs. I knew that the Foreign Office would be glad to hear the last of a matter which had caused them a good deal of worry during the past few years and accordingly, I was not surprised to find that they were quite willing to receive me. At a subsequent meeting, in which an Assistant Under Secretary took part, I produced my credentials and a print of my solicitors' letter to the Mining Company and explained the position from the Chinese point of view. Before I left I received an assurance that the Office would like to be kept thoroughly informed as to the course of negotiations.

Matters moved slowly at first as the Company contented itself with making an absurd counter-offer and progress was further delayed while the Board awaited the arrival of their General Manager who had been hastily summoned from China. But some advance was made at a meeting at which the Company's demand was reduced by £2,000,000. Finally, we reached a point at which only £100,000 or £200,000 divided the parties. And then, in November, the end came rather dramatically. The Company asked that before they decided on their final terms the Foreign Office should obtain information from H.M. Minister in Peking as to whether the Chinese Government still stood by its offer of Government Bonds. The reply was to the effect that the Chinese Government regretted that present financial conditions made the withdrawal of the offer compulsory. In January 1911, I received telegraphic instructions to return to China and, after a cordial exchange of farewells with the Department for Chinese Affairs, I left England. I had completely failed, but through no fault of my own. It was evident that after the return of the General Manager to China political machinery had been brought into operation with fatal results to our cause.

From April to November I was almost continuously in London, and visited the Foreign Office once or twice a week to report. On those occasions, I saw either the head of the Chinese Department, the Assistant Legal Adviser or (more rarely) an Assistant Under Secretary. I have good reason to be grateful to the head of the Chinese Department, who never grudged me his time and who earned my admiration by the cool correctness of his attitude. I had been told in April that the Foreign Office would put no pressure on the Company, and I was quite content to pour all the information I possessed into attentive ears, even if I received nothing in exchange. For I was allowed to feel that, if unsympathetic towards my clients, the Foreign Office was at least as anxious as they were to see the matter settled, and this helped to prevent my spirits from falling even during the darkest hours of these protracted negotiations.

During my stay in London, I had the honour of being invited, through the kindness of my London agent, who was a member of the Committee, to the Annual Dinner of the Law Society where I found myself sitting next to one of the partners in the firm which I had involuntarily assisted in 1902. It was an interesting meeting for both of us.

After my return to Shanghai, I had two or three cases in Hongkong before I went home on leave in 1913. I was now in a position to fix my fees at $400 and $200 (a leader's brief fee and refreshers) for all days in court; Tls. 100 a day for other days of absence from Shanghai; and my expenses. I felt obliged in common fairness to charge more than local men could claim and, although a local leader occasionally had $1,000 marked on his brief, that fee covered a lot of work which I never had to do. At any rate, my charge of Tls. 100 for days when I was not in Court was still enough in all conscience, seeing that they

T.M. Thorp

included six days of pleasant sea-faring. On one of my later visits, I was detained for two months in Hongkong, the period of my stay covering the Race Week and also a week of Chinese New Year holidays. Moreover the Chief Justice was only sitting on four days of the week, as the Puisne Judge was absent on leave and his work had to be attended to. So I do not think that the local Bar could accuse me of unfair competition. In one case, I actually got Piggott to reverse himself, to the amazement of all the members of the legal profession. My client was so surprised and delighted that he nearly wept! But his success, I am sorry to say, was of no value to him as the Chinese who had been held liable to pay him a large sum of money immediately went bankrupt. The case, however, was very useful to me personally. But the years between 1911 and 1913 are chiefly remembered by me in connection with the great rubber boom and the crash which followed it. Shares were funded up to 1,000% premium and the end of the boom came whenever speculative buyers at the top failed to take delivery from sellers who had also bought on speculation. The whole rubber share market collapsed, several companies faded out of existence, many reputations were blasted, huge sums were irretrievably lost, and peace did not return for some years. We had a great deal of troublesome and anxious work, which was well handled by Jones, who had become a partner in the firm shortly before Hanson's retirement in 1908.

When Sir Francis Piggott retired, in about 1912, he was succeeded by Sir William Rees Davies, who had at one time been member for a Welsh constituency and a secretary to Sir William Harcourt. The arrival of this judge greatly improved the atmosphere of the Court, and restored friendly relations between the Bench and Bar. He was notable for his reluctance to decide any matter until he was quite certain that the parties had said all that they desired to say. In this connection, I may mention that, on one occasion, I applied to him for a winding-up order against a company. The application was vigorously opposed and the Court sat thirty-two times before it made the order. I have been told that the hearing on appeal to the "Full Court" extended over more than twenty days at the end of which the winding-up order was confirmed. I am inclined to think that there was perhaps a greater expenditure of public time than the occasion demanded. It was always a pleasure to me to appear before Rees Davies, although the acoustic qualities of his court were bad and I never found it easy to make myself heard in it. But I felt that I could rely on the judge's determination to miss nothing and, in fact, when I had to consider his notes in connection with an appeal to the Privy Council I found them to be as full and accurate as I could possibly have wished them to be.

T.M. Thorp

I have referred to the Full Court in Hongkong, so I should explain here that in my early days, both at Hongkong and Shanghai, no judgment could be effectively appealed except by going to the Privy Council, for at both places the Appeal Court consisted of the Chief Justice and Puisne Judge, the latter of whom could not overrule a decision of his senior. But for a good many years an arrangement had been in force by which each court assisted the other by the loan of a judge, so that a real Court of Appeal could sit when required.

In 1912 I once more revisited Tientsin in connection with further developments of the Chinese Engineering and Mining Company business. The prudent management of the Company, anticipating the exhaustion of a mine in which three miles of underground haulage were already causing embarrassment, had financed the Lanchow Mining Company whose inexhaustible coalfields lay so conveniently adjacent, up to the point at which the latter Company's monetary situation practically forced it to conclude a working agreement with its creditors. This agreement was of a vague and provisional nature but it embodied arrangements for the drawing up of a more formal document at a later date. I was instructed to settle this formal agreement with the legal adviser of the British Company and, after two months of assiduous labour, during the course of which each of us was hampered at every turn by our respective clients, we arrived at a complete understanding as to the form of the draft. The meetings, however, which were held with a view to its approval and signature by the parties, led only to such acrimonious discussion as threatened a rupture of intercourse; so it was finally decided to adhere to the Provisional Agreement with slight modifications. Signatures were affixed in June and the Kai-lan Mining Administration has since operated to the satisfaction, I believe, of all parties. My work and that of my collaborator was entirely thrown away; but, for my own part, I had little reason to regret my absences from Shanghai, as I had a very pleasant time and was amply remunerated. On this occasion I charged our usual fee for work outside Shanghai, 100 Tls. per day and expenses, and had been absent for more than two months. If I was rather disappointed with the result of our joint efforts, at any rate the cloud had a silver lining.

I have mentioned that extra-territoriality sometimes leads to complications. A case which I had during this year affords a good example. While it should not have been possible under any Chinese Government for a Chinese subject in China to abandon his nationality without license, it was nevertheless comparatively easy for a Chinese born in Shanghai to obtain registration there, at the Portuguese Consulate, as a Portuguese citizen born at Macao, where there is a considerable population of Chinese race, but subjects of Portugal by birth in the Colony. A considerable sum had to be paid for a transformation, the effect of which was to remove the newly created citizen from the jurisdiction of the Mixed Court and incidentally from liability for his just debts. The Portuguese Court required all proceedings to be conducted in the Portuguese language, there were no Portuguese lawyers and a deposit of 25%, I think, of the claim had to be made before the court would entertain the matter. So with that proceedings were practically impossible.

A client of mine sued his compradore in the Mixed Court for a balance of account and the compradore pleaded Portuguese nationality. The Court, following the usual practice, declined jurisdiction. The compradore then sued my client in H.S.M. Supreme Court for commissions or something of that kind. Actions by foreigners are not tried there unless the plaintiff has filed a submission to the jurisdiction signed by the proper authority of the plaintiff's nationality, and the compradore's submission was signed by the Portuguese Consul General. I pointed out to de Sausmarez that as I held in my hand the pleadings in a Mixed Court case tried some three or four years earlier, in which the plaintiff and his brothers had all declared themselves to be

Chinese subjects born in Shanghai, there was obviously some misunderstanding which should be cleared up. The Chief Judge agreed with me and told the Plaintiff's counsel that he would require to be entirely satisfied as to the regularity of the submission before the case went further. We heard no more about it. But I wrote what I fear was an impertinent letter to the Portuguese Consul General asking him to be good enough to let me see a copy of his authority from the Chinese Government to change the nationality of Chinese born in Shanghai. I will add (*honoris causa*) that he did not reply.

Among the barristers who practised in Shanghai were several unusual characters about whom I will say a few words.

While I was Acting Crown Advocate an elderly man came to my office one day and asked me to move for his admission to the local Bar. He told me that he was a barrister but, as he did not happen to have his certificate of call at hand, nor was his name mentioned in the Law List, it was obvious that he could not be admitted without some previous enquiries, especially as he knew no one in Shanghai. He was also in the unfortunate position of being unable to obtain Consular registration owing to his having apparently no nationality. His father, he said, had been a Danish Consul, but as he himself was born out of Denmark he was not, according to Danish law, a Dane.

Nor did his call to the English Bar, if he had been called, entitle him to registration as a British subject, so that, for the moment, he was under Chinese jurisdiction. He seemed to be a respectable person so I took him to see de Sausmarez, who was sympathetic and promised that the Crown Advocate, who was returning from leave in a few days, would look into his case. His story must have been true in essentials, for after a time he was admitted to practice, and was registered at H.B.M. Consulate General as a "British protected person." I am afraid that he got very little business, although I did meet him once in a Supreme Court case. As time went on he seemed to become eccentric in his dress and behaviour, and it was not long before he died. He remains in my mind as a strange and rather tragic figure. How came it that a man of his age, fifty, I should think, was drifting about the East?

At one time, our Bar included a gentleman who had had the misfortune to be suspended from practising in Singapore. He had not done anything disgraceful, but, after some quarrel with an officer of the Court, had remarked, "I hate you, I hate you, I hate you!" The Chief Justice, on complaint made, had thought fit to impose the penalty of suspension. Our energetic Crown Advocate had overlooked the admission of this individual, having been absent, I suppose, when he was allowed to join the body of local practitioners, but felt bound, as soon as he had become acquainted with his history, to move that he should be struck off the roll of the Court. The motion, naturally, failed, indeed, I am not sure that, by the time it came on for hearing, the Singapore ban had not been removed. He was a handsome brainy creature of a fresh coloured Hebraic type, and Christ Church, Oxford, was responsible, I believe, for his early training. He never made good, and soon disappeared or died. I had to threaten once to report him to the Chief Judge for some irregular proceeding, but he tendered a becoming apology and I know of nothing else against him. I disliked, about equally, the kind of person that he was and the kind of treatment that he received in Singapore, and from the Crown Advocate. It is not a crime to hate a registrar, and although, no doubt, the open expression of such a feeling indicates a want of self-control, I am not satisfied that an isolated outburst proves unfitness for practice.

I was at home in 1913 and on my return in 1914 I found everyone talking about a new barrister, a Mr. Levinson, who would, I was told, make the rest of us look very small. During my absence he had taken over a business, both partners in which had died in quick succession; and, if his testimonials were genuine, there were grounds for saying that we were lucky to have such a colleague. My information about him came from an intelligent client upon whom he had made so favourable an impression that, from the way in which he spoke, I gathered that I was likely to lose a retainer before long. However, as soon as I had met the man in Chambers, I knew that I had no cause for anxiety. A few months later he took into partnership a young Hongkong solicitor who happened to be out of a job and all went well at first. But not for long. One day the youngster came to me in great distress. His partner had left Shanghai suddenly, informing him by letter that he intended to return soon. He had also drawn from the Hongkong and Shanghai Bank the whole of the firm's balance, which consisted almost entirely of deposits made by Chinese clients on account of costs and Court fees in pending cases. The Bank had treated him kindly and had advanced, on his personal security, the Court fees which had to be paid in order to keep actions alive. But only a small part of the sum due for the goodwill of the business had been handed over and no more money would be coming in except in connection with new matters; for the deposits carried off by Levinson simply represented so much work that had to be done by his partner without further remuneration. Levinson did not return, but his statement that he intended to do so caused additional embarrassments, for, until it was certain that he would not reappear, the

A Barrister in the Far East

vendors of the goodwill remained bound to recognise him as the purchaser and could not enter into a new arrangement with his partner. But before very long it became evident that Levinson would not and could not come back to Shanghai. Official investigation had shown that the fugitive was not Levinson, an English barrister, but a Russian Jew with another name and a black record. How he became possessed of the papers and testimonials, which he brought with him, for the deception of Shanghai, I never heard, for a thick veil of official secrecy, was thrown over the incidents of his career. He was struck off the roll and rumour was busy with his name for a long time, a favourite story being that he was shot during the War as a spy. I cannot imagine how he found his way into the good graces of so shrewd a man as my client.

Another member of the Bar had an even more *lurid* career. He was an Oxford man (Lincoln, I think) or, at any rate, was accepted as such by the Oxford and Cambridge Society, whose annual dinners he used to attend. He was also, undoubtedly, a crook. Soon after his admission he attracted attention by his irregular and unprofessional conduct, but it was impossible for the Crown Advocate to take any definite action against him on account of the insufficiency of the evidence. At last, however, he gave himself away and was prosecuted as an accomplice of Chinese in a forgery of Chinese Bank notes. Of this offence he was guilty enough and might, without injustice, have been convicted, although I must say that the requisite corroboration of the evidence of his associates in crime was not overwhelmingly strong. So he obtained an acquittal on technical grounds. Unabashed by this experience he continued to practice but, not long afterwards, was proved to have taken a large fee from a Chinese for work which he falsely alleged that he had performed and was struck off the roll. I have been told that he then became associated with Chinese Communists and assumed a Chinese name and Chinese dress. My last news of him was given to me by a traveller who recognised him on a steamer as a passenger from Hongkong to Singapore. He then bore a Chinese name and was wearing native clothes. My informant promptly wired the fact of his presence on board to the Singapore authorities who met him on his arrival and sent him back to Hongkong. He was rather a good-looking fellow, with red indian features and his manners, except in Court, were agreeable enough. In Court, he was violent, insolent and provocative.

Lastly, I will mention an interesting man, who practised for a good many years in Shanghai and ultimately died there. He had been at one time President of the Union at Cambridge and had brilliant abilities, which might have carried him far. I believe that, in addition to being a most accomplished advocate, he was a fully qualified actuary. When he started to practise by himself in Shanghai he had the good luck to be entrusted by the Crown Advocate, who was going on leave, with all the bad cases which that official had in hand, the good ones having been already turned over to my firm. He handled these hopeless affairs with considerable skill, taking every proper point in favour of his clients while never letting the Court suppose that, because he was putting up a stout fight, he was under the illusion that he had a winning case. The result was that when, later on, he came to deal with a better class of work, he had already secured the respect of the judges and met with a fair amount of deserved success. But he was a drug addict who went steadily and rapidly downhill to his death. I think that his mind, at one time, became unbalanced, for, after selling his interest in his business to his partner under a covenant not to practice in Shanghai for three years, he returned within a year from England and had to be restrained by injunction from violating his agreement. He carried his case to the Privy Council where he argued it in person, but the Board curtly and contemptuously dismissed the Appeal. I opposed him in several actions and can say that, although I always happened to be on the right side, he never allowed me to forget for a moment that I was facing a dangerous and resourceful adversary.

Soon after my return in 1914, the war broke out. My partner, Jones, and my senior managing clerk went home to serve, and both of them lost their lives. Another member of my staff joined up later, so my junior partner and I were left to carry on as best we could until 1919. Shanghai had its full share of local trouble owing to the well-intentioned but sometimes ill-directed activities of the Crown Advocate, whose anxiety to detect infringement of the Regulations against Trading with the Enemy led him to impute illegality to many transactions which were entirely innocent. Even the less blatant forms of patriotism could only maintain a struggling existence, unwarmed by the sun of official approval. It was my privilege during the first years of the war to render some assistance to clients of mine who were special objects of the Crown Advocate's attention. These clients owned the goodwill of a firm originally composed of British and German partners, from the latter of whom the British partners at once disassociated themselves and carried on their business throughout the war to the advantage of their country as they had a practical monopoly of the export trade in oil seeds. They were hampered in every possible way by interception of correspondence, detention of cargo and the like, but they held their heads high and came through their trials successfully. I shall always remember them as good fighters.

Overall, the Mixed Court of Shanghai functioned satisfactorily, but in cases involving Chinese government interests could not be relied on to resist official dictation. When China came into the War, she started at once to confiscate as much German property as possible and, in particular, the assets of the Deutsche Bank, which was put into compulsory liquidation. An Italian called Passeri was appointed liquidator and, after collecting a large sum from various debtors, he applied to the Mixed Court to fix his remuneration. He was awarded 5% of the sum collected, the Court being guided to some extent by a Hongkong Ordinance, which allowed a similar percentage to liquidators of enemy firms in the colony. The amount was duly paid into an account of the Municipal Council, which ordinarily received fines, deposits of security, etc., but before it could be paid out an order for payment had to be signed by the Magistrate who, on instructions from Peking, refused his signature. So Passeri never got his money which, by the way, he might probably have paid to himself without troubling the Court. But he was a formalist. Having stolen his money the Chinese Government proceeded to dismiss Passeri from his office, but ultimately paid him a small sum, less than 10% of his claim, so as to avoid trouble with the Italian government, which was inclined to take up his case. I admit that the liquidator's duties were not onerous, but they were faithfully and correctly performed and there was no legitimate excuse for the treatment accorded to him.

In 1916, I was engaged in the most troublesome case that I ever handled. My clients were an Indian firm of dealers in opium and they were sued by a Chinese plaintiff for the delivery of 200 chests of the drug. These chests were of enormous value, as the import into China of Indian opium had entirely ceased some years earlier. The entire imported stock belonging to foreign or Chinese dealers had been turned over to an organisation called the Opium Combine, which fixed selling prices for new businesses and delivered chests against the undischarged contracts of its members. The defence to the action was that the contract had been cancelled at the buyer's request when opium was at bedrock prices and the Combine had not yet been formed to support the market. The office staff of the defendant firm at the time of the alleged cancellation had all returned to India, so evidence had to be taken in that country on commission. After a long trial de Sausmarez decided in my favour.

The plaintiff appealed to the Full Court as then constituted (two judges) and, after filing his appeal motion, obtained a general search warrant against my clients on the ground that their manager had falsely denied the existence of certain books the entries in which, it was said, proved the plaintiff's case. Acting, as I believe, with the connivance of the manager, they raided my clients' office and obtained possession of books and documents. The manager came to me, and having reported the outrage, bolted to Japan. The plaintiff's solicitors next persuaded the Crown Advocate to have a Warrant issued for the manager's arrest on a charge of perjury, but they never attempted to execute it, although I am sure that they knew his hiding place. A new manager had to be sent from India to instruct me, and pending his arrival I proceeded against the plaintiff's solicitors for trespass, the issue of the search warrant having been manifestly irregular. I relied on the well-known old case of Wilkes and through that I was certain to succeed. The Assistant Judge, however, who tried the case, not only gave judgment against me, but lectured me severely upon the impropriety of my conduct in making allegations of bad behaviour against respected members of my profession. His criticism did not affect me because I knew that the right was on my side, but I began to think that in view of the official and other forces opposed to me I should be wise to seek for some outside assistance. Unluckily my friends, Messrs. Platt & Co., to whom I applied and who would have been glad to help me, felt obliged to remain neutral, as they had just refused a similar request from the plaintiff's solicitors. So I had to carry on alone.

I soon had to endure another blow, for just before the date set for hearing of the Appeal, my clients' new manager went mad in my office and died a day or two after his removal to hospital. It was with great difficulty that I obtained a postponement of the hearing until his place had been filled.

Among the documents discovered by the raiders was one which at first sight seemed to be very damaging to my case. This was a receipt signed by one of witnesses for a sum of no less than Tls. 60,000. I had been told nothing about this payment, and had merely advised that the man's evidence, though not essential, might prove useful. Some years before he had claimed ten chests of opium from the plaintiff, who had pleaded in the action that he was unable to deliver because my client had cancelled his contract. He produced in court the pleadings and a settlement drawn up by the present plaintiffs solicitors under which he got four out of his ten chests and he gave his evidence very clearly. He was not cross-examined, but, for some reason or another, the Chief Judge made no reference to him in his judgment. The explanation of this payment was very simple. The witness had suffered loss through our cancellation and thought that, if he helped to establish it for our benefit, he should get some compensation. This view of the matter was accepted as reasonable by the Assistant Judge at the hearing of the appeal and the Full Court had no hesitation in affirming de Sausmarez' judgment. The Chief Judge was very strong in his condemnation of the search warrant. A certain amount of new and suspicious evidence produced by the appellants rather damaged their chances. But what chiefly contributed to our success was the fact that the books which were found had never been disclosed to me and would obviously have been of great assistance to me if I had had the opportunity of using them.

An appeal to the Privy Council finally determined the case in our favour. Their Lordships, of course, strongly disapproved of the payment made to the witness, but they laid stress on the point that his evidence did not affect de Sausmarez' judgment and that the real matter in controversy, namely the cancellation of the contract, had been established by the decision of both the lower courts.

During the war, we had a good many cases with regard to delivery of opium. The drug was steadily rising in value and those firms by which it was held were subjected to constant attack by persons who claimed on various grounds to be entitled to delivery of a chest or chests. The Opium Combine had retained Messrs.

Platt & Co. to look after the interests of its members so Chinese claimants generally came to us for help. I was successful in winning several cases for them; but the defendants often preferred to settle out of court rather than to risk an adverse decision, which might affect the general interests of the Combine, which were valued at about Tls. 20,000,000. So things went on until one day very old clients of ours, who were members of the Combine, came and implored us to accept a retainer from that body. As they had ignored our existence for so long we were not prepared to agree except on very special terms: for acceptance meant that we should have to decline all future Chinese business affecting any of the members and might find that we had been simply immobilized and were not intended to do any active work. However, we decided after some consideration to fall in with the wishes of our friends and very soon received instructions to defend a heavy claim against them which we did with complete success, although I must say that the plaintiffs were shockingly advised. They were entitled (if anything) to opium from the Customs Bonded Warehouses and, although they had ample notice that the Chinese Government intended to close the Warehouses and take over the opium stored there by agreement with the owners, they had persisted in claiming opium already released from Bond. They amended their claim half way through the hearing: but, by that time, the Warehouses were closed for delivery and the Court held that their own misguided behaviour was entirely responsible for the defendants' inability to meet their new demands.

In 1918, a very important case engaged my attention for several months. The Oriental Cotton Spinning and Weaving Company Limited suffered loss through a fire at their mill and brought actions against three Insurance Companies on their policies. Two of the Companies paid without going to court, but the third, to the astonishment of all concerned, set up a defence of fraud, alleging that to the knowledge of the plaintiffs the goods claimed on were not, in fact, stored in the burnt premises. The charge of fraud directly impeached the honesty of the firm which managed the mill, and had, of course, to be met. Before the case was concluded de Sausmarez stopped me on the question of fraud and ultimately allowed part of our claim. But he never seemed really to get hold of our main point, which was that the iron hoops found by an independent witness among the debris and carefully counted, belonged, and could only have belonged, to burnt yarn, seeing that such hoops can never be stored but are made for the occasion and are cut and discarded when a bale is opened. To this day, I have never understood why we did not obtain a complete victory. During the course of the proceedings, the principal witness for the defendants, the man at whose instigation the charge of fraud had been put forward, gave a most astounding illustration of the extent to which veracity may be affected by prejudice. He swore that the hoops which had been found did not belong, as we said, to bales of the Company's own yarn, but to bales of Indian yarn of which we denied possession. This Indian yarn, he declared, had evidently been used in the mill and the hoops were there to prove it. After the court had adjourned it was explained to me that Indian yarn is never hooped but is made up into bales by means of a continuous metal band which is passed round the yarn two or three times; so that what the witness had sworn was not merely false but ludicrous. I went to the next hearing prepared for slaughter, but counsel for the defendants immediately applied that his witness should be permitted to make a correction in his evidence. The man then explained that he had made a mistake and justified himself by producing photographs which showed that bales of Indian yarn, if looked at end on or from one side appeared to be hooped, whereas, in fact, they were held together by a continuous strip of metal. He also apologised for having unintentionally misled the Court. This may seem to be a rather thin story, but it was good enough to take some of the sting out of my cross-examination and to make it possible for the defendant's counsel, later on, to treat his evidence as being due rather to blundering stupidity than to deliberate wickedness. Of course, he was entirely discredited as an expert, but he did not seem to mind that.

I earned a large fee in this case, which was one in which I felt the burden of responsibility more than ever before or since, until I was stopped on the question of fraud.

During the war I had to defend, at de Sausmarez' request, a young Indian who was charged with murder. A great deal of anti-British conspiracy among natives of India was being directed from British Columbia or Rangoon and strong countermeasures had to be taken, including the attachment to H.B.M. Consulate General of an important official of the Indian C.I.D. The accused had introduced himself into the Indian staff at Nanking of the International Export Company (a cold storage concern) with the object of killing another member of the staff, who was a secret agent of the British Government. He accomplished his aim, and having admitted and justified the act before the British Consul at Nanking, was sent to Shanghai for trial.

This young man, a fanatical revolutionary, for a long time refused to be defended, but at last consented; and I had several interviews with him at the gaol. He was very intelligent and had some education, but he was violently opposed to the British Raj and insisted that if I appeared on his behalf he should be allowed to make a statement in his own words. I was sure that he would merely boast of his crime, of which he was extremely proud, but I had to promise to obtain for him the privilege he demanded.

At the trial I had no difficulty in discrediting the evidence of alleged eye-witnesses and the Chief Judge told the jury to disregard it. But the confession was really an insuperable obstacle to acquittal. Nevertheless, I came pretty near to getting him off. I told the jury that he was, like them, a British subject, a citizen of a part of the Empire for which he had the same passionate love as they had for the part from which they came and for which they would be ready, like him, to give their lives – and so on. "Pause before you decide to cut short this young life!" But the foreman was a friend of mine whose common sense I knew only too well, and, as he told me later, though some of the jury were included to "wobble" at first, he soon steadied them up. The C.I.D. representative also confided to me that when the jury went out he was anxious about their verdict. But the prisoner's confession coupled with the statement which he made in Court duly brought him to the end which he deserved.

Just before I went home in 1919 for a short holiday I had an amusing case which could not, I think, have come to court in England. Besides the Shanghai Stock Exchange there existed another body of Stockbrokers called the Shanghai Stockbrokers Association which was registered like the Stock Exchange under the Companies Ordinances of Hongkong. The Chairman of the Association was a well-known and respected sportsman who always seemed to be rather out of place among his fellow members, and who had reason before long to regret his connection with them. The Association had difficulty in pulling through a settlement and the Chairman came to me for advice as to whether certain invested funds which, under a clause in the Memorandum, could be used for the benefit of the general body of members, might be used as security for a loan to help the settlement and obviate the necessity of a winding up. I advised him that these funds could probably not be used for such a purpose without a technical breach of trust by the directors, but that, if he and his colleagues on the Board felt bound to apply a dangerous remedy to a desperate case, they should protect themselves by getting all the members to sign a document promising to indemnify them against any ill consequences. He put my opinion before a General Meeting which was sitting to discuss the situation, obtained the necessary signatures, and in due course borrowed a sum sufficient to enable the Association to tide over the trouble. A few months later the Association took the amazing step of suing the

Chairman individually for breach of trust, although as a matter of fact he happened to be the only member who had not required or received any assistance in connection with his settlement. I defended, and naturally brought in the signatories of the indemnity by way of Inter-pleader and I got an order that the Chairman's claim against them should be heard as soon as the action against him was concluded. These preliminary operations took some time, but when it had once started, the case moved rapidly to the inevitable conclusion that if the Chairman had committed any breach of trust, which was doubtful, he was entitled to relief under the Trustee Acts. I had great fun with the witnesses, many of whom gave the impression, by their answers in the witness box, that Yiddish was a tongue more familiar to them than English. But I think the defendant won his case with the Chief Judge by his straightforward account of what had happened. He described briefly and clearly how the members were reduced to paralytic impotence by the threatened disaster, and how he had to undertake single-handed the task of trying to find some means of averting it. "When I came back to the meeting from Mr. McNeill's chambers, I found them sitting round, dumb, like a lot of penguins!"

I see that I have come nearly to the end of my story without having made any references to collision cases, except that of the Chishima and Ravenna. But I really had a good many of these cases and always enjoyed them. No amount of experience ever cured me of my optimistic belief in the yarns spun for me by my witnesses. Every sailor maintains that his ship was in the right and the other ship in the wrong and refuses to admit that there may perhaps have been faults on both sides. It is impossible to shake them out of a story to which they have once committed themselves and their obstinacy sometimes leads to disaster. I once had a perfectly good case against a steamer which had run down a junk. She had committed every possible mistake, including the faking of her log. But the judge was obliged to reject the junk's claim because her crew all swore that she was moored to one anchor with her head up stream, while a mass of independent evidence proved beyond doubt that she was under way, as she had a perfect right to be, and, if moored as alleged, must have been heading down stream. The pleadings in these cases always fascinated me owing to the topsy turvy way in which one side must sometimes refer to the facts connected with the collision. "The A with her stern struck the B on her port side just abaft the funnel culling her nearly to the water line," becomes "the B with her port side struck the A a heavy blow which twisted the stern of the A and otherwise caused her great damage." Both sides mean the same thing, but one has to say it upside down. One seldom, if ever, hears of a prosecution for perjury in connection with Admiralty cases, but very often the witnesses on one side give evidence which turns out to be quite inconsistent not only with all probabilities but with the fact of collision.

I have spoken before of the obstinacy of sailors, and two cases have since come to my mind in both of which I took part and in both of which one of the skippers concerned justified or rather attempted to justify a glaring error by reference to the same non-existent rule of the road. In each case it was contended that in the Shanghai River (the Whangpoo) which is tidal, ships proceeding with the tide have in all circumstances a right of way. There is no such rule, international or local, although it is obviously easier for a ship to slow down or stop when she is proceeding against the tide than when she has the tide in her favour. In the first case a ship coming in with the tide at night and intending to cross the main channel in order to reach the so-called "Ship Channel" which ran up to Shanghai along the opposite bank, saw another ship leaving the "Ship Channel" for the main channel and showing her red light. The incoming ship nevertheless came across, struck the other vessel on her port side, sunk her, and drowned nearly all her passengers. The only excuse was that the incoming ship had a right of way and was therefore, I suppose, justified in running down any steamer which had the temerity to shape an outward course along her own side of the channel. The Court, needless to say, did not accept this view; but I am quite sure that the master honestly believed that he was innocent of blame. The second case was an even more remarkable one. A British - India steamer was coming out from a wharf on the left bank of the river and was crossing to her proper side of the down river channel. While in mid-stream she saw a coasting steamer two miles off coming in with the tide, but after she had crossed over and had nearly straightened up on her course, this steamer ran into and damaged her. The master of the coaster was a particularly attractive sailor and as I cross-examined him at length I can say positively that he had no doubt whatever as to his ship being blameless because she had a "right of way". Yet all that he had to do in order to avoid collision was to keep to his own side of the channel without even necessarily reducing his speed. He was found solely responsible for the accident, but I was much struck by the honest simple way in which he put forward his mistaken views.

Another captain who held the same opinion in a less extreme form was, in my opinion, very hardly treated by Wilkinson. He started to bring his coaster in with the tide from an anchorage outside the mouth of the river as he was obliged to turn against the tide at Shanghai in order to get to his wharf. When starting he noticed two miles off the masts of a P. & O. steamer coming down the "Ship Channel". He knew that the two ships were likely to meet at about the point where the "Ship Channel" joined the main channel, so he decided that he would hug his own shore and not attempt to cross to the "Ship Channel" until the liner had passed him. But the P. & O. steamer, an old worn out tub, could not straighten up against the tide as she rounded into the main channel, but carried right across the river and sunk the coaster which was proceeding dead slow along the opposite bank. Wilkinson held that the coaster was to blame on the ground that in the circumstances she should never have left her anchorage, in which case, however, it must be noted that the P. & O. steamer would have gone very badly ashore. The vessel was owned by Chinese who promptly "sacked" the British master and he, poor man, took his position so much to heart that he went mad and died. This was, I think, without exception the most unreasonable and cruel decision that has ever come to my notice. If acted upon in general it would seriously have interfered with traffic on the river, and, as it was, it cost a decent sailor the loss of his employment and of his life. That the P. & O. steamer was also found to blame for numerous errors, which included the signalling that she was directing her course to starboard when she was in fact out of control, and swooping across the river to port, does not mitigate the defects of the judgment.

Broadly speaking the law of the sea is international, but in one matter I discovered to my annoyance that it is not. A Dutch steamer laden with oil and benzene went on fire just outside the mouth of the river and the municipal fire float, manned in those days by volunteer firemen, went twelve miles downstream to her assistance, and succeeded, with much difficulty, in saving the ship and part of her cargo. Several of the firemen were badly burned by exploding tins of benzene. The Municipal Council, as owners of the fire float, claimed salvage in the Dutch Consular Court, but the claim turned out not to be maintainable under Dutch law, which only awards compensation to individuals in respect of work done or injuries sustained, but not to the owners of craft or appliances used in salvage operations for services rendered. I was, as I say, annoyed, for it seemed to me that the provisions of the Dutch code ignored the principles on which the law of salvage is based, namely that salvors must be encouraged by the hope of liberal remuneration to risk life and property in salvage work. In this case the risk to both was great; but the decision had to be accepted, and I must add that the individual firemen were amply rewarded for their gallant work.

A strange place, Shanghai, and things happen there which could hardly happen anywhere else. For example, the incident described below.

Some years ago, an American baseball team came to Shanghai and played games against a visiting team from Tokio University and against the local club. The team was composed of members of a crack (coloured) regiment of cavalry and easily proved its superiority over both competitors. A final match was then arranged against the Japanese team and on this occasion the Cavalry were utterly defeated. The play of the U.S. team was so unsatisfactory in the opinion of experts that an official enquiry was instituted with the result that a young Jewish member of the Race Club was proved to have bribed the coloured players to "throw" the game and win him a large stake. He doggedly maintained his innocence and even threatened proceedings for libel against his critics; but he never dared to face a court and was expelled with ignominy from the Race Club.

Some years ago, a Manchester firm had a good market in China for piece goods and especially for certain cloth called "Lastings". Their 2 Bat Chop or ticket was very popular. Another Manchester firm noted the situation and sought to take advantage of it by introducing another 2 Bat Chop. But, whereas the original chop displayed two Bats, nearly as large as life, the new chop bore the Chinese characters meaning 2 Bats. It was hoped, no doubt, that if dealers writing from up-country ordered 2 Bat Lastings through Shanghai agents some at least of the orders might be carried out by a shipment of goods under the "character" instead of under the "animal" chop. The owners of the "animal" chop promptly commenced proceedings in Manchester for infringement of trademark and evidence had to be taken in China on commission. Bourne sat as Commissioner and I appeared before him for the plaintiffs. A great many "experts" were called for the defence principally for the purpose of proving the indisputable fact that the bat is, in China, a symbol of good luck and therefore to be seen in many chops. One of these "experts" was asked by me to look at some twenty or thirty tickets which had been put in by counsel for the defendants and all of which obviously contained bats, and to tell me what animals, if any, he could see on them. I do not know what was in his mind, but I suppose he thought that I wanted to trip him up somehow, for he persistently maintained that he could see no animals at all. "In one," he said at last, "I see a small creature which may perhaps be a bee." I was quite pleased with this irrelevant evidence, but my friend was not. We had a number of sittings and the costs of that commission must have been at least £1,000. I heard afterwards that the "character" chop people settled the case by paying £250 damages. I hope that they also paid the costs; for the attempt, although it failed, was fraudulent.

T.M. Thorp

In the summer of 1919, I went home for a few months and during my holiday took a first step towards retirement by purchasing a property in the county of Argyll. I came home again in 1921 and stayed from July to October to see how I liked my new home.

A case in which I had advised, and in which I had hoped to appear, was decided just before my return to Shanghai as it was a matter of urgency. It was an action against the Consul General in Canton for refusing to transfer a lot of land in Shameen - the British concession there - to a company registered under the Hongkong Companies' Ordinances, the members of which were all of Chinese race, although many of them (including the entire board of Directors) were Hongkong born British subjects. The refusal was due to a very natural desire to preserve an extremely limited area for the use of those for whose benefit it had originally been acquired by the British Government, but unfortunately, it was inconsistent with the terms of the Government leases which had been granted in times when company registration in Hongkong had not been even thought of. These leases provided that no transfer should be made (under penalty of forfeiture) to a "native of China", words which could not be said to apply to a British Company. And so the Court held. An appeal to the Privy Council was threatened but not proceeded with. The case was a bad one to fight as the transaction of sale had been completed some time previously and the purchase money had been paid over. The Consular authorities had not even a chance of success and the attitude which they adopted only resulted in considerable expenses being incurred by both parties. In my experience, British officials are too prone to defy the law when they think that they can do so with impunity for the purpose of attaining an object which is in their opinion beneficial and which cannot be otherwise attained.

One or two examples of this failing may be given. On one occasion, H.B.M. Consul General at Shanghai directed the Vice-Consul in charge of the Land Office to refuse transfer of certain Lots on the British Register which were being offered as prizes in a lottery conducted by an Italian and perfectly lawful according to the Italian code. I took the opinion of eminent counsel in London and, as I expected, he advised that the action of the Consul General was illegal, although, he added, it would be difficult to get a Court to interfere.

On another occasion H.M. Minister, acting under bad advice, published a Regulation requiring all share contracts made by British subjects to contain the numbers of the shares. This measure was intended to check excessive forward speculation and purported to be enacted under a provision of the China Orders in

Council by which H.B.M. Minister was given power to issue emergency King's Regulations for the maintenance of law and order. When a share-broker client of mine claimed a balance due from a constituent in respect of share transactions, this Regulation was pleaded in defence, but the Chief Judge accepted my argument that it was *ultra vires* the Minister to alter the English Law of Contract which only requires the numbers of shares to be inserted in contracts for the sale of Bank shares, and the plaintiff succeeded in his action.

I have always resisted to the best of my ability any attempt on the part of officials to arrogate to themselves powers, which properly belonged either to Courts of Justice or to the Legislature. For example, when I came to Shanghai in 1895 the real estate of a deceased person did not by law vest in his executors but in his heir-at-law, and land held in Shanghai under perpetual lease from the Chinese Government had been considered by the Court in Shanghai and by the Law Officers of the Crown in England to devolve as realty. But the Land Officers at the British Consulate always required the signature of transfers by the executors, and even objected to registering conveyances by heirs-at-law. Titles on the Consular register were, therefore, in rather a tangled state when, early in the present century, it was declared by a new Order in Council that land in Shanghai should devolve as personalty.

In another matter, also one of importance, the attitude of the Land Officers occasionally caused great inconvenience and real risk of loss to innocent parties. It was required by Order in Council that every mortgage of land by a British subject should be registered within a specified time at the British Consulate, against the lot or lots concerned. But the Land Officer refused to carry out such registration except in the case of mortgages by registered owners. A registered owner, however, might happen to be a trustee for another British subject who had in fact mortgaged the land, as he had a right to do, and was bound to register the charge to make it effective in favour of his mortgagee. Consequently, mortgagees were sometimes deprived of protection to which they were entitled and intending purchasers who inspected the register obtained no notice of an incumbrance on the property. We were more than once obliged to threaten to apply for a Mandamus, before we could induce these servants of the public to carry out their purely formal duty of recording transactions in a register. As I have cited particular examples of misbehaviour, I ought to say that the business of the Land Office was as a rule promptly and efficiently performed.

Towards the end of my time in China I had to deal with a rather curious case. The widow of a man who had been compradore to an Insurance Company, started twenty years ago to compete with the China Mutual, claimed 5% of all premiums earned by the Company since its inception, under the terms of an agreement entered into by her late husband with the promoters. I resisted the claim on the ground that the agreement had been cancelled by mutual consent almost as soon as it was made, and I was able to prove not only that the compradore had never claimed or been paid anything under it during his life-time, but that he had been borrowing large sums from the company almost up to the time of his death: these sums he had repaid with interest. But the plaintiff was a remarkably clever witness and nearly persuaded the judge that there was some substance in her claim. There was one point, however, which she was unable to get over. Her husband had for two years left the Company, which was just beginning to stand on its feet, and acted as an agent for its rival, the China Mutual, from whom he received commissions on policies taken out through him. He returned after a time to his original service, but it was impossible to contend that the agreement, if then alive, survived his departure, and there was no evidence that it was resuscitated after his return. In this case, I had to face a difficulty which sometimes embarrasses a defendant in countries like China. One of the promoters of the Company, an American, was visiting Shanghai, but was bound to return across the Pacific before the action could be tried. He did not want to be involved in the matter at all, as he had not a very good record to take with him into the witness box, but he was the only person who could give direct evidence for the defence as to the agreement and its cancellation, so I had to examine him *de bene esse* before the case came on. He was badly mauled by counsel for the plaintiff, but was, fortunately, unshaken on the few points that were of importance to me. It is most inconvenient to have to examine a necessary witness for the defence before you have heard the plaintiff's case, and especially a witness like this one, of first rate importance and tenth rate character.

In 1925, I was drawing close to the end of my professional career. Both my partners were getting on in years; and it was quite time that the top step should be left clear for them. For nearly twenty years, I had been the senior in my firm and, as I felt that I was in a position to retire, it was proper that I should do so. But I cannot say that I was in a hurry to go. I was not only useful to the firm in the capacity of a figure-head, but I advised the more important clients and handled most of the work of the Municipal Council, particularly in connection with agreements regulating the position of the Waterworks and other public utility companies. My position as a leader in Hongkong had been strengthened by a final success: for in 1923 I had conducted an important case there, and the Privy Council had upset the judgements of the Chief Justice and the Full Court and decided in favour of my clients. I might, therefore, have reasonably looked forward to ten more years of active work in Shanghai and Hongkong.

As a final incident of my practice, I represented the Municipal Council at what was known as the "Judicial Enquiry". The disturbances of May 1925 and the shooting by the Municipal Police of several rioters had led to the appointment of a tribunal, consisting of the Chief Justice of Hongkong (Sir Henry Gollan) a Justice of the Manila Supreme Court, and a Japanese judge, to go into the whole matter and apportion responsibility. I appeared with one of my staff, a barrister, for the Council, Macleod and another barrister (of Platt & Co.) represented the Commissioner of Police, whose conduct was impugned, and other counsel (solicitors) acted for the police sergeant who ordered the shooting, and for a Deputy Commissioner of Police who happened to have been very near to the spot when the trouble occurred.

I did not expect that I should have much to do, for it had never been seriously suggested that the Council was in any way to blame; but things turned out otherwise. The Tribunal directed me, on behalf of the Council, to lay before it all evidence in the possession of my clients which bore in any way upon the disturbances. As this intimation was given without warning, I obtained a short adjournment. But I foresaw great difficulties, as I was not permitted by those who represented the men directly implicated to see proofs of their evidence, while I knew that I should have to put before the Commissioners evidence which was in the hands of the Council and was likely to weaken any defences, which might be set up. The adjournment was short enough for all that we had to do in the way of obtaining proofs from eye-witnesses and other persons. Fortunately, my assistant was quick and intelligent and took much of this work off my shoulders. Then we had to arrange the order in which the facts were to be presented, and to get subpoenas for all unwilling witnesses. We had further to decide upon a general plan for presentation of an enormous mass of detail relating to the origin of the trouble. The question of "mob psychology" had also to be gone into with an expert, and I had to discuss at length with the Chairman of the Council the powers of the Council in relation to the police and in general. I cannot deny that the decision of the Tribunal was a practical and, from their point of view, a convenience one, but it seemed to me at first that I had been asked to perform an impossible task. The Commissioners, however, made due allowance for my difficulties, and my friends were not too obstructive when my duty obliged me to practically cross-examine their clients (nominally my own witnesses) on matters known to the Council, but not touched on in their evidence. I think that it was as difficult a bit of work as I have ever tackled, but I managed to carry it through somehow, and Gollan assured me before I sat down that I had fully complied with the wishes of the Tribunal. We had about ten sittings, several of which, naturally, were devoted to the evidence of the incriminated parties. The Tribunal allowed me to have them examined, in the first instance, by their own Counsel, who were also permitted to make speeches on their behalf. But no one who has not attempted it can realize the difficulty of presenting evidence merely as evidence and without suggesting that it proves anything in particular. That was, however, what I had to do: for the Council did not set out to establish a case but simply to aid the Tribunal in deciding on the questions submitted to it. No attempt, I may say, was made by any of the three men to shift responsibility from themselves to the Council. Macleod lightened my burden considerably by taking over as part of his client's case the evidence on "mob psychology" and the C.I.D. evidence as to Soviet activities, prior to the outbreak.

The finding of the majority of the Tribunal (British and Japanese) completely exonerated from blame both the Council and the three individuals whose conduct had been the subject of special investigation. When we sent in our Bill of Costs to the Council some of the members protested against the amount, and we agreed that there should be an informal reference to the Taxing Master of H.B.M. Supreme Court whose decision we were willing to accept. We were quite clear as to our position; for we had charged these old and valued clients in a matter of exceptional importance a sum representing about 20% less than we should ordinarily have charged in a Supreme Court case of similar character. So we simply itemized our bill (including the 20%) and got it allowed in full. Although we claimed and were entitled to no more than the amount originally demanded, I am glad to be able to record that the Council paid us the whole sum allowed by the Taxing Master.

I left China for good in February 1926 and resigned from my firm at the end of the same year, having completed more than thirty-five years of active work in the Far East. My doctor can find nothing wrong with my health, so I look forward without enthusiasm to what, for all I know, may be a lengthy period of complete, though by no means voluntary, idleness. I should have been glad to have been able to take a more active part in public life, but my connection with the Municipal Council compelled me to sit silent at meetings of Ratepayers; and I often envied the free lances of my profession their right to dispose of their services as they pleased: they may perhaps have lived from hand to mouth, but they knew more of the job of battle than did one who was tied, like myself, to the "big interests."

Before I left England, I never gave a thought to what I now regard as a most important question, namely the possible effect on my health of a change of climate. It happened, however, that when I came to insure my life on my marriage I found that my Insurance Company only charged me the home rate as long as I remained in Japan, although they put me up to the Indian level when I moved to China. Yet in Yokohama I saw a sight which I never saw in China - strong young foreigners absolutely crippled with rheumatism: and apparently no account was taken of the earthquake risk. After I had been in China for about ten years without any impairment of my health, my insurers were good enough to reduce my premium by a substantial amount. Both China, i.e., Shanghai, and Japan had climates which might fairly be called good. The summer heat was endurable and the winters, though sharp, were not severe. The commonest diseases were malaria, dysentery, typhoid and sprue [coeliac disease]: none of these touched me seriously. I suffered slightly from dysentery for one or two days, had a mild attack of typhoid, and (in 1912) a bout of malaria, which left no after effects and did not recur. But

I have learned from the experience of others that no one should go to live in Shanghai if he or she suffers from any weakness of the digestive organs.

Although during my first years in Shanghai I was kept very busy in the office, the firm took good care that I had enough time for recreation. If the partners worked late, as they often did, they always drove me away about five o'clock to get a round of golf or a few sets of tennis. I was soon roped in to row and play football, and before long stroked a Scottish eight which won the International Race against England and Ireland and captained a victorious eleven of the Shanghai Football Club in the great annual match with the Marine Engineers. Races at Shanghai were rowed in quite a different way to that in which I had been brought up, for the reason that young business men could not afford to row themselves out very often if they were to keep fit for their office work. So a race generally meant a brisk start, a strong paddle over three-quarters of the course and a bucket home. This system suited me very well as I found that I could often train my crews up to being able to cover their water at forty for about twenty strokes and that generally meant a comfortable lead which could be maintained at least up to the final spurt. Although I was never really good at any sport or game there were many forms of recreation from which, as a moderate performer, I got a great deal of amusement. Among these I may mention golf, tennis and clay-pigeon shooting. Golf I practically abandoned after 1901 as I acquired a houseboat and took to going up country at week-ends to shoot.

In the autumn of 1900, after the relief of the Legations, I went for a long shooting trip up the Yangtze in a friend's houseboat, which had come up by the Grand Canal, and spent three weeks in a creek about thirty miles upriver on the North bank. We saw a great many pheasant and being a lucky sportsman I managed to bag a wolf. There was a regular launch service from Chinkiang to the mouth of our creek so that, by the kindness of Messrs. Jardine Matheson & Co.'s agent, we were able to get our mails and occasional supply of milk and meat. The country was quite peaceful and apparently no one had heard of the Empress Dowager's flight from Peking. During most of this trip we kept very strange hours, as our watches got far ahead of the real time, and, when we started out before breakfast to look for a duck, we really began our day at 5 a.m. instead of at 7 as we thought. On the 5th November, we experienced a remarkable change of the weather, which had been so mild that we were always able to take a dip in the creek on our return from shooting. In the night, a violent wind blew us from our moorings and piled us up on the opposite bank, and in the morning we found the country frozen hard. About a week before our return to Chinkiang my friend's dog was badly hurt by a heron, and accidentally wounded through being in line with a snipe. The bird drove its bill clean through the dog's shoulder and he nearly bled to death. I shot badly, as I was using the gun which had been given to me when I was a boy and which no longer fitted me. When I sold this twenty years' old hammer gun at an auction, I got more for it than it had originally cost.

On my arrival in Shanghai, I joined the Volunteers as everyone else did. I had no strong call to this form of public service, but I took my duty seriously, and at the time of the Boxer outbreak had reached the rank of corporal and had command of a section of cyclists. The corps was brigaded with the British Second Brigade which remained in Shanghai throughout the trouble and, in due course, we all received the China medal. I passed my examination for a commission before a Board of army officers; but as our Company officers were chosen by election I was naturally beaten, on a vote, by my own sergeant who had also passed the Board. However, I succeeded him as sergeant and finished my six years of service in that rank. Nearly all the officers of the corps were men who were really keen on Volunteer work, and many spent their home leave doing courses at Wellington Barracks. I was not fit for commissioned rank, owing to my lack of genuine interest. Later on I commanded a company of reservists who were armed with shotguns and who did useful work in time of disturbance by relieving tired sentries. I never happened to be in Shanghai when my company was mobilized so that I can only speak of its performances from hearsay.

After I had bought a houseboat I used to go up country for almost every week-end from about the 20th August, when the snipe arrived on their way South, to the end of the first week in May when nearly every bird has flown to the Northern breeding grounds. I brought back, as a rule, very small bags - a pheasant, a duck, a few quail or snipe, a hare - that sort of thing - but I got away from my work and had a good walk on Saturday afternoon and Sunday. Later, when our children had gone home to school, my wife used to accompany me, as she enjoyed the walking and was very good at marking birds. On longer trips, we generally visited a mountainous district where, in addition to pheasants, I could get some bamboo partridges. These very beautiful birds are often found in coveys of twelve to fifteen and scatter widely when flushed. They do not fly far, so good marking helps the gun very much. I remember one pleasant trip to this locality when a friend and his wife came with us in their own houseboat and our bag may be cited as an example of the shooting to be had within a hundred miles of Shanghai twenty years ago. We got in ten broken days: twenty-five pheasants, sixty partridges, twenty-three woodcock, three deer, seven hares, thirty quail and twenty odds and ends - chiefly snipe and pigeon. Added to this were good weather, lovely scenery, and easy paths on the hills for the ladies.

Yet another enjoyable trip was made with another gun up the Tientang river. We travelled a hundred miles to Hangchow by houseboat in tow of a launch, crossed the city (six miles) in chairs, and embarked on the river in a native houseboat which we made comfortable with curtains and stoves. We shot for a hundred miles upstream and got over a hundred pheasant and thirty partridges, but we saw no other game. The partridges were being heavily trapped by the natives in any cover that was near a village. On this trip we were able to send a coolie from time to time to Hangchow with game for transmission to Shanghai by a missionary friend. Our messenger travelled on foot, and by boat, and our friend's name was held in such respect throughout a wide area that no one attempted to steal birds which were being conveyed to his house.

I used to enjoy the spring and autumn snipe shooting when it was so hot that one had to wear a sun hat; but a real objection to it was that nearly all the birds had to be thrown away, as they could hardly be kept fresh for one night except in the ice box, and neither the houseboat coolies nor the natives would eat them. I was lucky with snipe as with other birds for while many of my friends who have shot hundreds of snipe have never shot an albino, I got two in one season, one being a common snipe and one the larger bird which we knew as Swinhoe's snipe. I have also shot solitary snipe, which few Shanghai sportsmen have encountered, and Jack Snipe, which most old hands say is unknown in China. The shooting of the solitary snipe occurred on a hill about fifty miles from Shanghai. I and my companion saw two, and another party on the opposite side of the hill also saw two: three were bagged.

During my stay in Shanghai I was at one time or another president of the St. Andrews Society, the Rowing Club, the Gun Club (clay pigeons), the Oxford and Cambridge Society and the Bowling Alley Club - the last mentioned club was a very select institution consisting of but twenty-four members and had a club house and alleys of its own. Admission was by unanimous invitation, so that it was really an ideal club, all the members being intimate friends. I spent many pleasant hours there and had the reputation of being the most regular attendant. In my last years, after I had sold my house, I lived for some time with an ardent yachtsman and at his instigation joined the Midget Sailing Club, whose members sailed small boats on a creek fifty miles from Shanghai during week-ends from April to June and in September and October. I had a good boat, which won me many races, and I became, before long, the club's Rear-Commodore. This also was a delightful club to belong to and I shall not forget the good times we had.

We used to live at week-ends on our houseboats, of which five or six were kept permanently moored beside the course during the season. As a rule, we left Shanghai on Saturday by a 12.30 train, lunched on our boats at about 1.30 and pottered about under sail during the afternoon. Then on Sunday we brought off half a dozen races, a convenient train taking us back to Shanghai in time for dinner. We always entertained on Sunday a lot of visitors who arrived at breakfast time either to take part in the races (we had several spare boats) or to look on.

The best day I remember was one on which we had a two-reef breeze and boats had to carry three men or capsize at once. None of the seven boats that raced had any accident, which I think creditable to the club. The Chinese authorities have recently stopped this harmless sport, although the country people welcomed our visits and made a good deal of money out of us in one way or another.

The year 1925 (my last in China) was a very disturbed one, but real trouble did not break out in Shanghai until May, when the shooting, to which I have already referred, took place. We were all up country at a Rowing Club Regatta which was held on the same creek as that on which we sailed, and on Sunday volunteers and police were recalled to Shanghai. Later houseboat parties were directed to return on Monday by a non-stop special train, and were advised to keep heads down for fear of missiles. Fortunately, a motor houseboat, which was attending the regatta, had a wireless installation so that the return of the service men and others was managed without difficulty. Our servants behaved splendidly and carried on as if nothing had happened. All was quiet in Shanghai when we arrived, but for three months not a Chinese soup was open nor were the lives of foreigners safe except in the heavily patrolled main roads. The whole Volunteer Corps was mobilised, sailors and marines were landed from the men-of-war and Shanghai was in a state of siege. Most Chinese in foreign employ went out on strike, and the electricity works and waterworks were run mainly by Russian refugees of whom there was fortunately a good supply. Many business firms temporarily lost all their Chinese staff, and many families their domestic servants. The Shanghai Club was kept open with some difficulty by the members, with the assistance of ladies who kindly attended to the bedrooms. No shipping moved on the river.

In my office we kept all our Chinese, who were well rewarded later for their loyalty. I can also say the same of my domestic staff. My chauffeur left me at once, as he was a corporal in some kind of armed force organised by the strikers, but he sent me an efficient substitute and returned when the situation became normal. I asked no questions. Business so far as my firm was concerned was more or less hung up, as my young assistants were out for most of the day and night with the Reserve Police.

I had rather an interesting time myself, for the man who was then commanding the Shotgun Unit detailed me as one of the guards of a motor canteen run by the British Women's Association which took refreshments round at night to the armed posts. The American women ran a similar canteen and the ward was divided by arrangement so that there was no overlapping. The British canteen used to start from the office of the Hongkong and Shanghai Bank on the Bund, where a room had been put at the disposal of the Association, at 9 p.m. and return at 1 a.m. to replenish stores. At 2 a.m. a new round was begun which finished at about 6.30 or 7 a.m. I and the Scandinavian who was then messing with me volunteered for the second journey as, being older men, we were less embarrassed by the hours of duty. At first we were out every night, but when further men were detailed for the work we had one night on and one night off: later we had two nights off. The ladies began by serving all night, but soon found it necessary to arrange that those who started out at 9 o'clock should be relieved on their return to headquarters. The canteens supplied sandwiches, doughnuts, coffee or cocoa, and cigarettes, which were paid for out of the funds of the Associations, and they always carried a few bottles of aerated water for any Sikh policeman they might happen to meet. The work of handing out coffee and cocoa and washing cups was hard: but the men were very grateful. One most efficient canteen worker told me that the American Marines sent her a bouquet of flowers every morning. My friend and I soon became used to getting up at 1.15 a.m. and, as my boy always called us punctually, we never arrived late at the Bank. Occasionally if we reached home before 7 o'clock we could snatch an extra hour of sleep but, as a rule, we had to be content with what we got before we started on our four mile drive into town. My mess-mate always went with the American canteen which worked the outlying districts near our house, so he was able to drop off when the work was finished and the canteen was ready for its return journey.

I have already described the disturbances in Shanghai of 1925; the only other riot with which I had anything to do was the so-called "Wheel-barrow Riot" of 1897. In that year the Volunteer Corps was suddenly mobilized one day about noon and the members lost their luncheons. A mob of wheelbarrow coolies had come into the International Settlement across the Creek which then divided it from the French Settlement, had broken some windows of the club, and stoned some of the members. The reason for their violent behaviour was that they objected to a proposed increase in the licensing fee for barrows, which, in those days, were the ordinary means of conveyance for native passengers and for cargo. There was really no rioting after the first brisk half hour, but the Corps was kept under arms for two days, its duty being to patrol the roads near the creek and the bridges leading into French territory. I found the affair quite amusing, as I had the "good" hours - 10 to 2 - and so, while I did no office work, I was able to breakfast before going to my post, to lunch not too late, to dine at leisure, and to enjoy grilled bones at the Club before drifting home to bed.

In addition to the Volunteers some British blue-jackets and marines for a time gave protection to life and property; but the consular body soon insisted on the Municipal Council postponing the increase of the tax for three months, the principal native official, the Taotai [Intendant of Circuit] having made himself responsible for a cessation of disturbances if postponement was agreed to, and also for payment of fees on the new scale when it came into force; so the corps was demobilized and - for Shanghai is a strange place - a meeting of ratepayers was immediately called to censure the Council for having tamely yielded to consular pressure. Many passionate speeches were delivered and a vote of censure was passed by a huge majority. The Council of which my future partner, Dowdall, was a member, at once resigned. The criticism levelled at them was unfair and even absurd; for they were practically compelled to accept the official suggestion. If they had rejected it they would have lost the support of the British Navy and would have made themselves responsible for any resulting damage.

The police did not often trouble us in the matter of Mixed Court prosecutions, but in my last year I was called in to deal with a Dr. Fortunatoff, a Russian who was nominally attached as physician to the Soviet Consulate-General at Shanghai but who was really, according to my instructions, one of the lading members of the Cheka [Soviet state security agency] in China. Some documents incriminating a prominent Soviet propagandist had been found in his steamer cabin by a White Russian member of the Municipal Police force, and Fortunatoff was accused of attempting to bribe this man to say that the papers which he professed to have discovered were forgeries deposited by himself among the passenger's baggage on the instructions of his superiors. The policeman reported to headquarters and a trap was laid for Fortunatoff, who was arrested while in the act of handing over the bribe. I spent much time in getting up this case, but when I arrived at the Mixed Court for the trial I was told that Fortunatoff had fled. I never heard of him again and I do not know how much of my instructions, except of course as to the actual arrest and the matters directly connected with it, was based on fact and how much on White Russian prejudice. I wish that the case had been tried.

In the first decade of the present century we were instructed by the Admiral commanding the U.S. Fleet on the China Station to appear before arbitrators on behalf of a naval collier which had been in collision. She was found solely to blame. We presented our Bill of Costs which was certified by the Judge of H.M. Supreme Court and approved by the Admiral, under whose directions we forwarded it to the Navy Department for payment. The Department, however, expressed regret that it had no funds at its disposal which it could allocate to the payment of legal expenses and advised an application to the Attorney General's Department. Here again we were met with a *non possumus*, the Attorney General stating that it was beyond his powers to pay for work which had not been done under his instructions. Neither the Admiral nor two of his successors were able to do anything to help us although they gave us their fullest sympathy, but after a year or more of ineffectual efforts on our part, the Attorney General or the Navy Department at length promised that a Bill should be presented to Congress authorizing the payment of our costs. The promise was kept and the Bill was duly approved by the appropriate committee, but it was never considered by the House owing to its adjournment. Next year the process was repeated, but again our Bill had to give precedence to other legislation and was never reached, while the House was in Session. As we were getting no nearer to receiving payment we addressed ourselves to H.M. Minister in Peking, who, after a few months, informed us that the matter had been placed in the hands of H.M. Ambassador in Washington. Our hopes rose, but they were again doomed to disappointment and another year passed without our obtaining any satisfaction. It was now nearly four years since we had done our work and we had begun to despair of success when it occurred to me that a former Secretary of Legation in Peking, with whom I had had some dealings, was not attached to the Washington Embassy. I wrote him a personal letter, telling him the facts, and asking for his assistance and received a most kind reply. Not long afterwards the much belated payment was made by some Department or other, and although we lost a good deal on exchange, we were very glad to have heard the last of this troublesome affair.

In 1925, just before I went home, I appeared in a very interesting case concerning a man named Ingenohl. He was a brother of the well-known German Admiral who commanded the High Seas Fleet at the beginning of the War, but had himself, ten or twelve years before 1914, been naturalized as a Belgian. He carried on an important tobacco business in Antwerp, and also owned, at the outbreak of the War, a cigar factory in Manila, as well as certain trademarks under which were sold the best known brands of Manila cigars. These trademarks were registered in Hongkong and China and elsewhere throughout the world. In 1919, that is to say after the Armistice, the American custodian in Manila of enemy property confiscated and sold all Ingenohl's property and rights in the Philippines on the ground that he was a German. It did not take Ingenohl very long to establish his Belgian nationality or to recover the sum paid by the purchaser, but American War legislation prevented him from getting back his property, as titles derived from the custodian were declared to be indefeasible. But it was by no means clear that the American authorities had power to affect Ingenohl's rights except within the limits of the Philippines, and in particular to prevent him from selling cigars under the marks which he himself had invented in his principal markets of Hongkong and China. So Ingenohl started an action in Hongkong in which he established his right to his trademarks registered there and, encouraged by this success, sued in Shanghai for an injunction to restrain a British

Company, which was the agent of the purchaser, from selling cigars under his marks in China. I hoped that I had won this case for Ingenohl. My opponent certainly thought so at the conclusion of the hearing, and, while the Judge was considering his judgment, his clients were busy arranging with the agent for the marketing of cigars under new tickets, which were to replace those derived from Ingenohl. But the Chief Judge decided against me and, though the grounds of his judgment were, I believe, questionable, the Privy Council upheld it. The Board based its decision on a proposition which I can both understand and appreciate, namely that a Court should give to the War legislation of allied countries the widest possible construction. Holding these views, their Lordships were able to distinguish Ingenohl's case from the well-known Chartreuse case in which the monks of the Chartreuse were held to be entitled to all their rights, including the use of their trademarks, outside of France, although their property in France and their business of manufacturing liqueurs had been sold by order of the French government.

I was surprised that neither Court showed any sympathy for Ingenohl whose case was surely a hard one. He was admittedly the victim of a mistake, and was therefore morally entitled to any relief from its consequences, which could be granted to him within the strict limits of the law. One must, I suppose, assume the good faith of the American custodian, but it is certainly remarkable (1) that Ingenohl's nationality should have been mistaken after his long connection with the Philippines; (2) that no official enquiry was made regarding it; (3) that action was only taken after the Armistice; (4) that the purchaser was an insolvent cigar factory largely indebted to two powerful American Banks which immediately placed it in liquidation; and (5) that the sale was made at a gross under-value.

I will conclude by mentioning a case, which has no serious features at all. A little monthly paper called "The Rattle", which circulated for a short time in Shanghai and other Treaty Ports, was owned by J.O.P. Bland, H.W.G. Hayter (now, alas, dead) and myself. Our professed object was to extract as much fun as possible from people and events for the benefit of our readers without hurting anybody's feelings, and I do not think that we gave offence to any reasonable person. But there are some individuals whose exaggerated sensibility prompts them to find insult in the most unlikely places. That was how this trouble arose. One of our contributions was a resident in Chefoo, a small port with a reputation for bickering. He was not himself directly involved in any local squabbles, but most of his friends belonged to one of the two factions which were then engaged in fierce controversy over some trivial question, while the two persons whom I am about to mention belonged to the other, and consequently regarded our friend as a suspicious character. As a lighthouse construction engineer, in the service of the Chinese Maritime Customs, he had had considerable experience of foreign communities in similar small centres and had been an amused observer of their habits. So he sent us a lively article in which he described a purely imaginary election of Municipal Councillors at which all the eligible ratepayers, numbering eleven, presented themselves as candidates for nine vacancies and went on to state that, when these had been duly filled, "the other two went out and swore enmity to the powers that be over the Club bar." The two men referred to above considered that they had been insulted by the passage which I have underlined, and they commenced proceedings for libel against the writer. Of course, I had to take a hand in the matter and, as the pleadings merely set out the words complained of, and contained no innuendo connecting them with the plaintiffs or attaching to them any defamatory meaning, I thought that I had better go to Chefoo, where the action had been started in H.B.M. Consular Court, and try to get the Consul to strike out the claim on the ground that it disclosed no cause of action. The journey by steamer took two days, and I remember being rather pleased with myself for being such a good sailor, for there was a heavy head sea and the ship was "flying light"; only the Scottish engineer and myself (the only passenger) appearing at meals. On arrival, I took up my quarters with the Defendant and his family, and so began a lasting friendship. It did not take me long to file a motion with the Consul and to arrange for an early hearing. It was important, absurd though the case was, to smash it before it got into the papers, for no one could tell how Sir Robert Hart (the Inspector General of Customs) would take it; and the members of the friendly faction - though prepared to swear, if necessary, that they had neither understood the article as referring to Chefoo nor the passage complained of to the plaintiffs - were not very anxious to go into Court, and further embitter the existing feud. In due course the motion came on to be heard and I explained to the Consul, who naturally knew no law, some elementary principles of the law of libel. He quickly grasped, with the assistance of Odgers, the point about the innuendo, and very properly urged the plaintiffs to amend their claim by adding a definite statement that the passage set out in it referred to them, and by unveiling the insult which the writer had so skilfully concealed. Otherwise, he said, the case could not proceed. The plaintiffs stoutly refused to make any amendment, and the Consul's judgment was that if they did not amend within a month, the action should stand dismissed. I went back to Shanghai and the matter was never heard of again, except of course that the plaintiffs had to be worried until they paid the defendant's costs.

Early in 1926, my wife arrived in company with my barrister son who was joining the firm as an assistant. My intention was to remain in Shanghai until I retired at the end of the year, but it was considered to be more convenient that I should go on leave at once as another partner was taking a holiday in 1927 and our simultaneous departure would have involved too sudden a weakening of the firm's staff. So, after many farewell feasts, my wife and I left Shanghai for good in February 1926. On the way home I had the satisfaction of reading in the Times that my last case in Hongkong had resulted in the final success of my clients in the Privy Council - a pleasant ending to my professional life.

www.ingramcontent.com/pod-product-compliance
Lightning Source LLC
Chambersburg PA
CBHW030301100526
44590CB00012B/469